Good Practice Guide

Fees

Peter Farrall and
Stephen Brookhouse

RIBA ## Publishing

RIBA Publishing, 2021

Published by RIBA Publishing, 66 Portland Place, London, W1B 1AD

ISBN 978 1 859 46930 9

The rights of Peter Farrall and Stephen Brookhouse to be identified as the Authors of this Work have been asserted in accordance with the Copyright, Designs and Patents Act 1988 sections 77 and 78.

All rights reserved. No part of this publication may be reproduced, stored in a retrieval system, or transmitted, in any form or by any means, electronic, mechanical, photocopying, recording or otherwise, without prior permission of the copyright owner.

British Library Cataloguing-in-Publication Data
A catalogue record for this book is available from the British Library.

Commissioning Editor: Alex White
Assistant Editor: Clare Holloway
Production: Richard Blackburn
Cover design by Design by S-T Ltd
Designed by Studio Kalinka
Typeset by Academic + Technical, Bristol
Printed and bound by Page Bros, Norwich

Image credits
Figure 2.1 Stephen Brookhouse; Figures 3.1–4 RIBA; Figures 3.5–6, 4.1, 8.1–2 Peter Farrall

While every effort has been made to check the accuracy and quality of the information given in this publication, neither the Authors nor the Publisher accept any responsibility for the subsequent use of this information, for any errors or omissions that it may contain, or for any misunderstandings arising from it.

www.ribapublishing.com

MIX
Paper from responsible sources
FSC® C023114

Contents

	About the authors	V
	Acknowledgments	VII
	Introduction	IX
1	Procurement, risk and the role of the architect	1
2	Professional services contracts	17
3	Office finances and charge out rates	31
4	Fee calculation and negotiation: how to put together an effective fee proposal	43
5	Resourcing and systems for effective time management	63
6	Monitoring projects, change control and managing fees	73
7	Invoicing and cash flow	83
8	Putting it into practice: a case study	99
9	Summary	115
	Index	121

About the authors

Peter Farrall is a senior lecturer at the University of Liverpool, where he is responsible for professional studies as well as being a studio tutor on the BA and MArch courses. Prior to his current position, he was a partner in a small multidisciplinary practice in Chester, specialising in the education sector. He has also worked for two large practices dealing with commercial and residential projects. He is past president of the Liverpool Architectural Society, served on the National Council and Conduct Committee of the RIBA, and acts as an examiner for the RIBA Part 3 in the UK and abroad. He delivers lectures for RIBA Part 3 and CPD programmes.

Stephen Brookhouse is Professor of Professional Practice in Architecture at the University of Westminster in London. He is a chartered architect with over 30 years' experience as a director in commercial practice and professional teaching. He is a former non-executive member of the ARB Board, the ARB Professional Conduct Committee and the ARB Investigations Panel. He is also an accredited mediator. He lectures widely on professional issues in the UK and internationally and contributes to the RIBA CPD programmes. He has authored the *Part 3 Handbook* and *Professional Studies in Architecture*.

Acknowledgments

We very much want to acknowledge all the comments, suggestions, experience and insights offered by the chartered architects who attended the national RIBA CPD Programme and the other professional events we were invited to participate in. This feedback acted as a 'road test' for the principles and techniques that have now been further developed in the book.

We also wish to acknowledge the time and expertise given freely by the architects and other professionals who contributed to the content of the book, who shared their specific experiences – many of which are summarised in the cautionary tales – and who challenged us to add value to this essential part of architectural practice.

Introduction

This guide is the result of the authors' participation in the national RIBA CPD Programme on the topic of architects' fees. We quickly realised that, while the wealth and variety of experience and practice within the profession is huge, there is a common concern about the way the market for our professional services has changed and diversified. We need therefore to focus on and articulate the value of our services, and to reflect that value in how we charge for our services. Writing this guide has given us the opportunity to explore in greater depth the key issues raised by practitioners about their professional work and their businesses and to capture some cautionary tales, as well as to offer insights into good practice.

The guide is written for that vast majority of architects in practice in the United Kingdom who are either sole practitioners or work in micro- or small practices and whose clients are, in the main, domestic end-users. These projects are often categorised as relatively small in scale, but scale does not equate to simplicity. Rather, most architects in this sector work for what are demanding clients on highly complex projects that just happen to be small in scale. Within this vital part of the profession there exists a huge range of experience and skills. There are, for instance, architects who adapt and extend buildings, design new ones or work on historic and heritage projects, all within an increasingly complex regulatory environment, while at the same time providing specialist consultancy services. Architects also work across many different sectors. These range from education to leisure and include developer-led projects. Clients can be charities, housing associations, universities and local authorities. In consequence, architects manage risks – which are often not fully acknowledged. In doing so, they add considerable value. The main aim of this guide is to make the case for a clear link between the value you as an architect add to a project and the financial recognition of that value in your professional fees.

The guide starts by looking at how the scope of our services is impacted by different procurement routes and project risks. We then consider the importance of getting the right professional services contract in place; one that recognises the scope and value of an architect's services. This is followed by a review of finance, resource-based fee calculation and how to negotiate. Techniques for monitoring and managing resources are presented to help you keep your services on track. The importance of regular invoicing is emphasised, together with charging for partial services and changes to the scope of services. How to manage payment is also discussed. Finally, the key messages are applied to a case study.

The changing landscape of architectural practice

It is often said that architectural practice is becoming an ever more competitive environment. It is probably more accurate to say that the procurement landscape for projects has changed. Combined with ever increasing client expectations, this has had a significant effect on the way we architects practise.

Historically, architects have followed a traditional, linear 'general contracting' procurement model. This offered a full service from beginning to end. The architect was the main client contact, managed the design team and administered the building contract. This model informed the original RIBA Plan of Work, created in 1963 and adapted over subsequent years until its final version in 2007, which was then superseded by the RIBA Plan of Work 2013. Today, a majority of smaller scale projects are still procured using standard traditional building contracts. However, architects also now work in different roles and at various stages on design and build projects and developer-led projects. The annual RIBA Business Benchmarking survey of Chartered Practices shows that, these days, architects offer a wide range of services, including partial services, in a variety of roles. Even when following the traditional project procurement route, the architect may not necessarily be the lead consultant or contract administrator. The diversity of practice, changing roles and the scope of services are all reflected in the latest RIBA Plan of Work 2020 – an iterative rather than linear model of project delivery.

The number of stakeholders in a project has grown and the regulatory environment has become more complex. Clients recognise that architects are highly trained and talented; however, they expect transparency and to know how, where and when we add real value in a consumer-led environment. Unlike most other professions, architects work closely in a long-term professional relationship with clients as part of a team. Sometimes the services of an architect are seen as discretionary. If architects fail to differentiate sufficiently the value of the services they offer, clients will go elsewhere to achieve similar results or will expect the architect to be more competitive in terms of pricing and delivery.

If architectural practices continue to charge for services in the same way they have always done, it is reasonable to predict that their income will remain the same. However, given the trend over past decades, it is more likely they will find themselves doing the same – or more – for less. When you overlay both the increased complexity of the regulatory environment and the competition resulting from alternative procurement routes on top of higher client expectations, it is more likely still that the pressure exerted on fees will be even greater.

Business models must be sustainable and able to meet future challenges.

Our method

There are five simple steps that can be taken to link the estimated time and resources spent on a project with the agreed outputs and your costs:

1. Prepare a draft Project Resources Programme for your services across all or some of the RIBA Plan of Work stages that can be used with the different procurement routes.
2. Use the Project Resources Programme to identify agreed outputs.
3. Calculate your true costs and break-even point. Apply these to the time resource in your Project Resources Programme to get a baseline cost for the project.
4. Add a contingency for risks and unknowns plus an estimate of your value or profit.
5. Then you iterate. Plan for different scenarios and carry out a reality check – your fee has to be competitive.

If it helps, translate your estimated resource-based fee into a percentage of the estimated construction cost (your client may also have requested a percentage fee). The method recommended here is not the traditional 'finger in the air' percentage fee approach, but instead links revenue directly with cost and takes account of project risk.

It is worth reflecting on whether the percentage of construction cost method of charging for our services has served the profession well. The main problem with calculating your fee as a percentage of construction cost (apart, that is, from deciding what is meant by 'construction cost') is that there is no direct link between your actual costs and revenue. When you add in the complexity of different procurement routes, the varied roles of the architect and partial services at different stages and 'unknowns', the percentage fee suddenly comes to look like a blunt tool and a risky way to build a revenue model. Recognising that different methods can be and are used, this guide discusses three alternative ways of charging – percentage, lump sum and time-based charges – and the risks associated with each.

Revenue, cost and risk

This guide does not set out to tell you how to run your business, or how to manage costs or, for example, how to invest for future growth. It looks instead primarily at revenue. It highlights the need to build a revenue model using true practice costs as a starting point, thereby creating a clear link between cost and revenue. It looks at the connection between time spent, time to invoice, time to receive payment and the effect on your working capital. Monitoring and controlling resources are key business functions. There is no silver bullet. Instead, this guide explores the positive effect on a practice's profitability of the incremental improvements that result from regular monitoring and control.

Not all projects go to plan and some may incur losses. Monitoring and control can help in mitigating such losses when they occur. Ultimately, you want a business that is rewarding, professional and sustainable. It is important to be able to invest in the future of your practice and plan for improvements to your revenue stream.

Architectural practices operate at the sharp end of complex and costly projects that are of great value to clients. Design decisions exert leverage on project outcomes and no two projects are the same. An architect's role is often to act as the risk manager, in addition to adding value through design. One of the major challenges for practitioners is to take account of risks when planning the allocation of resources – and therefore costs – at an early stage, when the unknowns are greatest.

Your professional services contract

A professional services contract – that is, your agreement with the client – is the key building block of your business. Chapter 2 reviews the different types and forms of contract. A key point is that an architect's relationship with a client is long-term and complex. In a traditional project, this relationship will be formed, and the fees agreed, at the time of greatest uncertainty in the life of a project. In contrast, a 'package delivery' professional services contract with a developer-contractor can be well defined with relatively low levels of risk. It is important to assess these different types of risk and take account of them in your contract.

Throughout the guide, the value you bring to a project, and when and where that might be at its greatest, is emphasised. A long-in-the-tooth architect was once asked by a client how long it had taken him to prepare the design just presented; his answer was: 'About 30 years!' The same applies to newly qualified architects who have already dedicated ten-plus years to their career. The value that you bring through your knowledge, talent and experience needs to be recognised in the contract with your client. That said, any agreement with your client must also be of mutual benefit – the client needs to understand the inherent risks and the value you bring to a project at the different stages and you in turn need to understand the client's objectives. The Project Resources Programme and scope of services are key tools in communicating with your client, particularly with a domestic, end-user client. Monitoring your time against the Programme and scope will allow you to communicate effectively with the client when change occurs, as it almost inevitably will.

A challenging future

The context for practice has always been changing and challenging. Two factors have, however, remained relatively constant in recent years: the increasing complexity of the industry – how buildings are procured and the drive for greater efficiencies in delivery – and ever greater client expectations of the professional services we provide.

There are three other key factors that are becoming more significant and will have an impact on the scope and content of an architect's services:

- climate change
- the safety of buildings
- the wellbeing of users.

Each is a welcome development; however, each also brings challenges.

First, the breadth and depth of knowledge and the skills required for each project will change and grow. Second, there is likely to be a more complex regulatory framework in terms of sustainable development and building design, performance and use. In short, greater demands will be placed on the profession. Through a collective, professional commitment to CPD, time can be invested in acquiring the knowledge and skills necessary to meet these challenges and ensure that value is added. The widening scope of an architect's professional services must be to the mutual benefit of client and architect alike and must be reflected in our professional relationships.

1

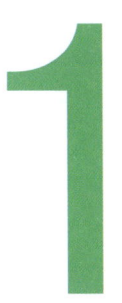

Procurement, risk and the role of the architect

This chapter gives an overview of the different procurement routes you are likely to encounter in practice. Understanding these different routes and the associated project risks is important because the procurement choice determines how risks are allocated, the different roles carried out and when they are undertaken. Including project risks, this determines the scope of services, when they are delivered and for how much.

The topics covered by this chapter include:

- the RIBA Plan of Work 2020 and the different roles of the architect
- project risks and risk management
- the procurement landscape.

Procurement

Procurement in its widest sense is the process of taking an initial idea from your client, agreeing terms and then taking the project through to completion and eventual use. Practice typically involves working for many types of client – from domestic clients commissioning a project for the first time to developers who understand the risks entailed in a construction project.

When considering the scope of your professional services, it is worth first putting yourself in the client's place and thinking about the wider meaning of procurement and project risks. Depending on how experienced the client is and the type of project, it is unlikely that the brief and project outcomes (what services are required, the fee and schedule) will be defined at the initial meeting to discuss the project.

You may work in a traditional procurement environment – one where the architect acts for and represents the client throughout every stage of the project – or you may work exclusively for either developer clients or contractor clients. You might consider that you know all there is to know about the different procurement routes. You may not, however, have thought systematically about project characteristics, or about risks and the ways they can affect how you plan your resources while still making a profit.

The characteristics of a project are also important. The clearer the project outcomes, timescale, boundaries and scope, the lower the perceived risks and uncertainty in terms of the professional services required and the time period needed for their delivery. This is important – time is a key resource. The scope of services and the time and effort needed to commit to a project must be estimated, defined and agreed. Without clear boundaries, the estimated scope of services and the resources allocated may be insufficient to fulfil the final project outcomes.

Poor communication at the outset makes it harder to manage client expectations. Without clarity at this stage, the scope and amount of services required are liable to grow. Furthermore, the time taken to deliver services without an overall Project Resources Programme can accumulate, often for reasons beyond your control. The fee may become stretched more thinly as a consequence, especially if there is no direct link between resources and fee (for example, if the fee is calculated according to the cost of construction). Later chapters explore further how to manage these critical early stages to ensure that the fees match the project outcomes and resources required.

The RIBA Plan of Work 2020 and the roles of the architect

The RIBA Plan of Work provides a recognised structure that can be customised to suit your needs. The roles defined in the RIBA Plan of Work are important as they align with the headline roles defined in the RIBA Professional Services Contracts (PSCs). They also delineate the various roles that architects are asked to undertake, as distinct from the all-encompassing professional service traditionally provided on a percentage basis. It is strongly recommended that you use the RIBA Plan of Work 2020.

Procurement, risk and the role of the architect

> **THE RIBA PLAN OF WORK 2020 ROLES**
>
> **Client adviser** – a consultant who provides strategic or specialist advice, particularly during the early stages of a project.
>
> **Architect** – responsible for carrying out the architectural design.
>
> **Project manager** – responsible for managing all aspects of the project and ensuring that the project is delivered in accordance with the project programme.
>
> **Lead designer** – responsible for managing all aspects of the design, including the coordination of the design and the integration of the specialist subcontractors' design.
>
> **Contract administrator** – responsible for the administration of the building contract, including the issuing of instructions and certificates.
>
> **Health and safety adviser** – responsible for health and safety aspects, as defined by legislation and in line with other project objectives.

Setting out your project roles is crucial. You also need to make the client aware of any other additional roles and consultants that may be required. These may include: cost consultancy; structural engineering; mechanical, electrical and plumbing (MEP) engineering; surveys; and specialist advisers, such as heritage and planning consultants. You should inform the client of any other services you provide in addition to your normal 'basic services'. It is essential that you brief the client on their statutory duties under the Construction (Design and Management) Regulations 2015 (CDM Regulations), particularly regarding the requirement for a principal designer on any project.

Generic roles can be linked to each procurement route, as shown later in the chapter.

Project risks and risk management

> The aim of engaging in construction is to take calculated risks. The life-blood of any business is to make money by dealing with the risks that others do not want to bear ... we should make risks explicit so that rational decisions can be taken about who should bear them.[1]

Construction projects, whether small, medium or large, are characterised by uncertainty, complexity and fluidity. Significant change is a natural part of the project lifecycle. It is a common misconception that small projects are somehow less complex or less fluid. All projects require you to manage significant change and unforeseen events. Further, every project is a prototype, even when sharing many characteristics with other projects. Experiencing uncertainty and complexity means encountering risks. This increases the likelihood of things not going to plan and the impact felt when it happens.

Project teams can be described as temporary, multi-party organisations. Even small projects have many stakeholders. As well as the client, there are the contractors, the design consultants, specialist contractors, direct suppliers, installers and regulators such as development control, conservation and building control. These add to the complexity – regardless of scale or value – and can affect the programme and delivery. The different procurement routes are intended to manage project risks in different ways.

What are the risks?

Some project risks can be controlled, some cannot. Some can be predicted, some are unforeseen. The main risks you are likely to encounter are listed below. This does not include major global risks to the wider economy or unexpected political events. The list is intended to help you estimate the impact project risks are likely to have on the project itself and on your services. Alerting clients to risks in a structured way is a valuable precursor to a project's Strategic Definition (Stage 0) and Preparation and Briefing (Stage 1). Not all of these risks will apply, but a checklist is useful.

PROJECT RISKS

Client risks (all RIBA Plan of Work stages)

- multiple clients and stakeholders – leading to inconsistency and delay, and multiple channels of communication
- ill-defined client objectives and requirements – leading to poorly defined scope (fluidity)
- lack of experience and knowledge – resulting in a lack of clarity and ill-defined objectives
- multiple changes to requirements at different stages
- ill-defined project budget
- delays to decision-making approvals
- cancellation – leading to abortive design work and cost.

Site risks (Stage 1)

- incomplete site information 1: boundaries, services below and above ground; legal issues: easements, restrictive covenants, wayleaves, party walls
- incomplete site information 2: survey information: physical, condition of existing buildings, condition of services, asbestos and issues that may affect health and safety, scope and programme
- location: restricted access and working restrictions.

Design risks (Stages 1 to 4)

- ill-defined brief and cost plan
- inappropriate selection of the design team
- delay in the overall project programme
- over-optimistic programme affecting either all or some RIBA Plan of Work stages
- incomplete pre-contract design
- technical complexity and novelty in design
- inadequate coordination of design information and incomplete technical design – pre-tender
- health and safety
- abortive or additional design work due to cost reviews (all stages, but particularly Stage 4).

Cost risks

- escalation due to changes in scope
- market changes at tender stage
- specialist elements
- cost reduction and abortive/additional work.

Regulatory risks

- town planning and conservation requirements
- delay to decision-making
- additional work in connection with changes

- risks associated with discharging planning conditions or reserved matters
- building control – inadequate information
- additional health and safety requirements.

Contractor risks (Stages 3 and 4)

- inadequate selection process
- inadequate information – tendering process
- lack of clarity on contractor-designed elements and design scope
- multiple direct client contracts for supply and installation
- specialist and/or single sources – MEP services and materials.

Construction risks (Stage 5): contract performance

- unforeseen events: ground conditions, asbestos, condition of existing structures, etc.
- contractor performance and management
- client changes leading to abortive and additional design and administration
- incomplete information
- constructability
- cost – increase
- programme – delay
- subcontractor performance
- quality issues – leading to additional administrative work
- additions to and omissions from contract requirements
- claims and disputes – cost, requirements and time
- defects and rectification period.

Health and safety risks

- potential regulatory issues
- potential cost and delay.

Procurement, risk and the role of the architect

How do we manage these risks?

The process of managing risks can be formalised by the preparation of a basic risk register. This is of use at the early pre-project stage as a way of informing the approach you take to the fee proposal(s). It can then be referred to later at regular intervals.

You should first estimate the likelihood of any risk and its impact on the project – in particular, the effect it might have on your services in terms of resources and time – before selecting a strategy or action.

Among the risk management strategies that can be adopted are:

- avoid – decline the project
- accept and manage – manage the risk effectively
- transfer – move risks to another stakeholder (e.g. specialist design)
- share – work collaboratively to reduce likelihood and impact.

Alternative procurement routes have been developed in response to different ways of managing project risks:

- design risk – responds to the risk of changes during the construction phase; and, increasingly,
- contract performance – responds to the risks pertaining to requirements, cost and time.

Clients have attitudes to project risk that range from risk averse to risk-taking. You need to be aware of the ways risks can affect how you manage the different key stakeholders in a project, especially design risk and project performance risk. Architects have traditionally acted as risk managers for clients, especially in relation to design and regulatory risks – two key areas where architects add real value to a project.

Contractors have developed relatively sophisticated ways of managing risk. It is also a commercial truism that if you accept a risk, you charge a premium for that acceptance. This tends to drive the contractor's approach to procurement and contract. The professional services contract and the building contract used by architects are both ways of expressing and agreeing a risk transfer or risk sharing with key stakeholders, who are normally the client, the architect and the contractor.

The procurement landscape

There are four main procurement routes:

- traditional or general contracting
- design and build
- management
- collaborative.

The two encountered most often by architects in a small or medium-sized conventional practice are: (1) traditional or general contracting and (2) design and build. Depending on the sectors in which your practice operates, you may also have come across variants, such as developer-led projects and framework agreements, which cover a variety of procurement routes. The different routes are described briefly below and the relevant RIBA Plan of Work roles listed. This will help in defining both the scope of services and how to charge for them.

Traditional or general contracting

Traditional or general contracting is the procurement route used most widely in general architectural practice. Contractually, the client (employer) takes most risks, including the design and cost risks, and the contractor takes the construction and contract performance risks. This is where the architect acts as risk manager for the client. In effect, the client transfers the design and project risks to you as the architect and you provide continuity through the whole project process and at each RIBA Plan of Work stage, from design to completion. You manage the design development and the design team, navigate through the regulatory landscape, accommodate change and act as contract administrator.

A characteristic of traditional procurement contracts is how they are able to accommodate changes to client requirements (i.e. fluidity). This can lead to changes being made during Stage 5 that affect contract performance. Programme delay, cost escalation, abortive work or potential confusion around changes in requirements can result in claims and disputes. Perceived as low-risk, the traditional procurement route can in some circumstances actually represent a high risk to the client precisely because of its fluidity. That is not to say that it should be avoided, but it is important to anticipate these risks when setting out your services to the client.

The RIBA Plan of Work roles for traditional or general contracting are as follows:

Core services:

- client adviser

Procurement, risk and the role of the architect

- architect
- project manager
- lead designer
- contract administrator.

Other services:

- principal designer.

Examples of the forms of contract typically used in traditional or general contracting are as follows:

Construction contracts:

- JCT Standard Building Contract, JCT Intermediate Building Contract, JCT Minor Works Building Contract
- RIBA forms of building contract.

Professional services contracts:

- RIBA Professional Services Contract
- bespoke forms (including letter contracts).

Design and build

In design and build procurement, the design risk is transferred from the client to the contractor. There is no single definition of design and build, nor the scope of services delivered to the client or contractor. Its attraction for clients is that the contractor accepts the design risks and can be appointed early in the project. However, as a result, the opportunities for the client to control the selection of specialists and change the requirements and design are more restricted. The architect no longer provides the continuity that typifies traditional procurement nor acts as the contract administrator. As the contractor accepts the design and contract performance risks and assumes control of them, there is potentially greater cost and time certainty – although at a premium.

The architect has three possible roles within design and build procurement:

- **Novation** – acting first for the client and then for the contractor

  The architect first acts in the traditional role of the client's architect until the contractor is appointed. The architect is then novated to the contractor for the remaining RIBA Plan of Work stages. Note that the architect works for the contractor post-novation – not the original client. The contractor is now your client. You will have a new appointment with the contractor. Contractually, the contractor (through the novation agreement) accepts all the risks associated with the work carried out before their appointment, as well as assuming responsibility for the future design.

- **Consultant switch** – working for the contractor

    The architect is appointed directly by the contractor (possibly without any prior appointment by the commissioning client) for the relevant RIBA Plan of Work stages under the design and build contract. This gives the contractor complete control over the selection of the design team and future design development.

- **Client representative** – working for the client

    The architect acts as the client's consultant during all the RIBA Plan of Work stages of the project. The architect works on the early stages and then acts as client representative during the design and build contract stages.

The RIBA Plan of Work roles for design and build are as follows:

Pre-novation:

- client adviser
- architect
- lead designer
- project manager (unlikely).

Other services:

- principal designer.

Post-novation:

- contractor's architect
- contractor's lead designer.

Consultant switch:

- contractor's architect
- contractor's lead designer.

Client adviser:

- client adviser
- architect
- project manager (possibly)
- lead designer.

Procurement, risk and the role of the architect

Other services:

- principal designer.

Examples of the forms of contract typically used in design and build contracting are as follows:

Construction contracts:

- JCT Design and Build Contract, JCT Major Project Construction Contract
- bespoke forms.

Professional services contracts:

- RIBA Professional Services Contract
- bespoke forms.

Developer-led projects

Developer-led projects effectively follow the design and build route where the developer is both client and contractor, and the architect is appointed to carry out various services over a range of RIBA Plan of Work stages. The developer is responsible for all aspects of contract performance and assumes all design and performance risks. Roles and responsibilities are potentially clearer, although much depends on how the architect is contracted to carry out the work and the way the wider project is managed in terms of scope and programme.

Examples of the forms of contract typically used on developer-led projects are as follows:

Construction contracts:

- developer-led project clients will usually use contracts they are familiar with – often bespoke forms – and which suit their business model.

Professional services contracts:

- RIBA Professional Services Contract
- bespoke forms.

Management

Management procurement falls into two categories:

- management contracting
- construction management.

Management contracting is identical to traditional contracting, except that in this case the contractor is appointed at an earlier stage. The aim is for the design team and client to benefit from early contractor involvement in design development and market testing. This helps avoid the risk of any post-tender redesign and changes to requirements (value engineering) in order to achieve the target budget. It allows project performance, cost and design risks to be managed at an earlier stage. It can also include significant design and build elements. The architect's role is very similar to the one in the traditional route.

The RIBA Plan of Work roles for management contracting are as follows:

Core services:

- client adviser
- architect
- project manager
- lead designer
- contract administrator (less likely).

Other services:

- principal designer.

Examples of the forms of contract typically used in management contracting are as follows:

Construction contracts:

- JCT Management Building Contract, JCT Management Works Contract, JCT Management Works Contractor/Employer Agreement.

Services contracts:

- RIBA Professional Services Contract
- bespoke forms.

Construction management breaks the project down into a series of major packages, each having its own direct contract with the client. The client appoints a construction manager as a consultant to manage the package contracts. The client assumes all the design and performance risks.

The RIBA Plan of Work roles for construction management are as follows:

Core services:

- client adviser

Procurement, risk and the role of the architect

- architect
- lead designer.

Other services:

- principal designer.

Examples of the forms of contract typically used in construction management are as follows:

Construction contracts:

- JCT Construction Management Appointment, JCT Construction Management Trade Contract.

Professional services contracts:

- RIBA Professional Services Contract
- bespoke forms.

Collaborative

The collaborative route to procurement represents a less adversarial approach where all stakeholders are encouraged to collaborate and work together in a spirit of mutual trust and cooperation. Risks are either shared or reside with whoever can manage them best. The idea of partnership in the project extends to creating longer term relationships where benefits are shared, with the potential for creating greater value for all stakeholders, as well as reducing cost. The collaborative route is an approach to project delivery that can include traditional, design and build, and management procurement.

Framework agreements

Framework agreements grew out of the collaborative approach to procurement. They are based on the perceived benefits of long-term relationships. A collaborative approach to risk management, with the potential to increase value and reduce cost through longer term relationships, is attractive to risk-averse stakeholders who procure projects regularly, such as local and central government, universities, part publicly funded organisations and charities. As a procurement structure and process, framework agreements are also attractive to private sector clients who regularly commission (similar) projects, whether they be retail, commercial, industrial or residential.
The procurement structure for construction projects will often mirror the client's own established practices for managing supply chain relationships. This is particularly the case in the industrial and retail sectors, where cost-effective supplier relationships are a key part of the sector business model.

Examples of the forms of contract typically used in the collaborative procurement route are as follows:

Construction contracts:

- JCT Constructing Excellence Contract
- NEC4 Engineering and Construction Contract
- bespoke forms.

Professional services contracts:

- RIBA Professional Services Contract
- NEC4 Professional Service Contract
- bespoke forms.

Summary

As a major stakeholder in the procurement of a project, you should consider your services in the context of the risks you manage on behalf of your client and the value you bring to a project as an architect.

Different procurement routes allocate project risks in different ways. Traditional procurement may at first appear relatively risk-free. However, the client (employer) generally takes all the design risk and leaves the contractor with the contract performance risks; for example, constructing the works to time for an agreed contract sum and in accordance with the contract documentation. Through the professional services appointment, the client effectively transfers many of the risks to the architect – the design risk in particular. There are several risks beyond the control of an architect. However, you may find yourself effectively taking ownership of many of them without recourse to a satisfactory method for dealing with the consequences in terms of time and resources – or without charging an adequate premium. Keep this in mind when negotiating your fee.

Design and build and developer-led projects can be less fluid and more secure because the risk allocation and management are much clearer. While the RIBA Plan of Work stages may vary, the services can be well-defined. By their nature, design and build contracts limit change, even though significant amounts of redesign work might be necessary to meet revised budgets. Timescales are also usually clearer. Other procurement routes can have characteristics in common with both the traditional and design and build routes.

You can make your own assessment of the project risks and how they might affect you in terms of resources and time. This can be done by creating a simple risk register using the risk lists above, relating them to the RIBA Plan of Work stages.

> **WATCH POINTS**
>
> - Identify a project's characteristics in terms of stakeholder complexity and experience, project complexity, clarity of objectives and fluidity: the definition (or otherwise) of project boundaries in terms of cost and time.
> - Carry out a basic risk assessment before preparing a fee proposal.
> - Consider the effects that the procurement route might have on the scope of your services and project timescales.

Endnote

1   Hughes, W, Champion, R and Murdoch, J. *Construction Contracts: Law and Management*, 5th edition (London: Routledge, 2015), pp. 94–95.

2

Professional services contracts

The contract you have with your client lies at the heart of your business. It sets out what your client can expect from you and what in return you will be paid, and when. If there is a lack of clarity or a serious omission in either the scope or the terms, there is a risk that the relationship will falter or, at worst, fail. As it determines the payment in return for your services, it is vital the contract reflects fully the resources and time allocated, the value that you contribute and the risks accepted.

The fee proposal made to a client must be right for the project concerned. It is very difficult to renegotiate services in the absence of clear project boundaries in terms of scope, time and risk. This chapter encourages you to consider and understand the following:

- your professional services contract as a 'project' with critical stages
- the profession's minimum requirements for a professional services contract
- the effect project characteristics and procurement route have on the scope of services
- the different types of contract that exist for your professional services – including standard professional services contracts
- how to include provisions to vary your fee.

Good Practice Guide: Fees

A complex relationship

Clients, especially consumer clients, want a professional architect who will guide them through the complexities, uncertainties, fluidity and risks of a project. The relationship may start informally and then develop along professional lines. The boundaries of the project – and hence your services – may be unclear at the early stages (Stage 0 or Stage 1). The relationship will be a long one and there may be multiple stakeholders. At times, it may appear more important than the tasks performed. This is because the obligations we begin to develop are, in effect, both relationship-based and task-based. The challenge is to formally capture the tasks – scope and performance – and to cement the relationship with the client. This requires us to manage fluidity and reduce uncertainty by following a set of formal steps.

The professional services contract as a project

The professional services contract crystallises the client–architect relationship and is the key element of your business model. It is helpful to consider it as a project in itself, with a beginning, a middle and an end (Figure 2.1). It is not simply a set of deliverables. This process takes place regardless of the procurement route chosen.

1. Pre-contract	2. Contract	3. Contract performance	4. Post-contract
Relationship-building	Agreed terms of the professional services contract	Carrying out the agreed services by the architect	Liability period stated in the contract
Agreeing the scope, deliverables and programme	The defined scope of services	Invoicing	Stage 7 services
Fee proposal	Fees	Monitoring	
Negotiation	Programme	Regular payment for agreed services by the client	
	Payment terms	Completion	
	Subconsultancies		

Figure 2.1: Diagram of the contract process: pre-contract, contract, contract performance and post-contract

Professional services contracts

1. At the **pre-contract** stage, you are forming a client relationship. This comprises discussions about scope and timescales, fees and risk apportionment. At this stage, you will need to translate this relationship-building into a formal fee proposal for the delivery of the professional services proposed to meet the client's requirements. You may be in competition with other architects at this pre-contract stage. The fee proposal may lead to further negotiations and possibly a pre-contract letter of intent (see below). You may also decide not to continue the relationship.

2. The **contract** stage is when the terms of the professional services contract are agreed. This should be seen as distinct from the earlier pre-contract stage. The contract sets out the obligations you and your client have agreed to undertake. It confirms the agreed performance by the architect and the client – i.e. you agree to carry out a set of services within a timescale for a fee (or fees) and the client agrees to pay the agreed amount(s) at agreed intervals.

    If there is a failure to meet the obligations and the contract has been breached, either party can seek damages in a court of law. In English law, courts rely on the contract agreed between the parties as setting out their respective obligations to each other. The contract should therefore accurately record obligations and avoid any omissions or ambiguity that could give rise to misunderstandings and possible disputes.

    It follows that the less formal the contract is (a basic letter contract, for example), the greater the risk that it will lack clarity, even in defining the scope of the services and setting out the payment obligations for the performance of those services. The greatest risk lies with an oral contract or in correspondence that may be relied upon as a contract in the absence of a formal contract, such as letters of intent, letters of comfort or letters that make reference to contract terms but neither state nor include them. These types of contract regularly result in formal complaints by clients to both the RIBA and the Architects Registration Board (ARB), particularly as regards the scope of services, payment terms and disputes.

3. **Contract performance** is effectively fulfilling the obligations agreed in the contract. The services are carried out to an agreed programme and the client pays for the services on schedule. The Project Resources Programme explored later in the book is a key tool for planning project performance against time. As well as a plan for calculating fees, it can be used as a tool for monitoring performance and, where applicable, as an aid to renegotiating or amending fees, should the scope of your services or timescales change.

4. The **post-contract** stage covers the liabilities and period agreed in the contract and this should be recognised in your fee. (This includes limits to your liability and liability periods and collateral warranties that extend your contractual liability to others.)

The requirements of the profession

The profession recognises that an oral agreement is insufficient to fully reflect an architect's obligations to a client, due to the complexity, value and worth of an architect's service. The RIBA and the ARB set out the minimum requirements for a professional services contract. These are shown below, with the key elements relating to fees highlighted.

THE RIBA CODE OF PROFESSIONAL CONDUCT 2019

Principle 2: Competence

2. Terms of Appointment

   2.1 All terms of appointment between a Member and their client must be clear, agreed and recorded in writing before the commencement of any professional services.

   2.2 Members must ensure that the terms of that appointment cover the key requirements of a professional services contract, including where relevant:

   (a) definitions;

   (b) architect's services ;

   (c) client's responsibilities ;

   (d) assignment;

   (e) fees and expenses ;

   (f) copyright licence;

   (g) liability and insurance;

   (h) suspension or termination;

   (i) dispute resolution; and

   (j) the consumer's right to cancel.

   2.3 Members shall ensure that any variation to a standard form of contract is clear, agreed with the client and documented in writing. The fact that the standard terms have been varied must be clearly stated on the document.

   2.4 Members shall ensure that any subsequent variations to the terms of their appointment are agreed with the client, clear and recorded in writing.[1]

Professional services contracts

> **ARB: THE ARCHITECTS CODE: STANDARDS OF PROFESSIONAL CONDUCT AND PRACTICE (2017)**
>
> *Standard 4: Competent management of your business*
>
> 4.4 You are expected to ensure that before you undertake any professional work you have entered into a written agreement with the client which adequately covers:
>
> - the contracting parties;
> - the scope of the work;
> - the fee or method of calculating it;
> - who will be responsible for what;
> - any constraints or limitations on the responsibilities of the parties;
> - the provisions for suspension or termination of the agreement, including any legal rights of cancellation;
> - a statement that you have adequate and appropriate insurance cover as specified by ARB;
> - the existence of any Alternative Dispute Resolution schemes that the contract is subject to and how they might be accessed;
> - that you have a complaints-handling procedure available on request;
> - that you are registered with the Architects Registration Board and that you are subject to this Code.
>
> 4.5 Any agreed variations to the written agreement should be recorded in writing.[2]

Consumer clients

Many small and medium-sized practices gain most of their work from consumer clients. The consumer in English law has a different set of rights to those of commercial clients. It is not the purpose of this guide to provide detailed legal guidance on consumer rights. However, if your client is a 'consumer' as defined by the Consumer Rights Act 2015 (CRA 2015), it is strongly recommended you meet your client to go through *each and every* contract term. Failure to do so could lead to the contract being invalid.

Going through the contract with your client is also is an invaluable opportunity to confirm the project details, explain your services and fee, and answer questions. This stops any misunderstandings before they escalate into disagreements or disputes. It also helps manage the client's expectations of the services you propose in order to meet the project's requirements.

Pre-contract: assessing the characteristics before you agree the contract

As a key stakeholder in the procurement process, an architect's services are inextricably aligned to the characteristics of construction projects (as identified in Chapter 1). These are, in particular, their fluidity, uncertainty, risk, complexity, the numbers of stakeholders and, if pre-determined, the procurement route. You should make a preliminary assessment of these characteristics before calculating your fees.

Time

Consider the *total* estimated, proposed or agreed project timescales across all the relevant RIBA Plan of Work stages. This will vary according to the procurement route chosen – from Stages 0 to 6 (or 7) for traditional procurement to specific Plan of Work stages for other procurement routes. As you assess the requirements of a project, it makes good sense as a first step to draft a Project Resources Programme covering the relevant Plan of Work stages. This is to enable you to set out the scope of your services and estimate the resources required. How to do this effectively is discussed later in the guide and it will form the basis of your fee proposal.

Standard professional services contracts: the RIBA suite

The RIBA has published a set of RIBA Professional Services Contracts (PSCs), updated to take account of stakeholder feedback, changes in legislation (particularly the CDM Regulations and the CRA 2015), relevant contract case law and up-to-date legal advice.[3]

The contracts align with the RIBA Plan of Work stages. Practices involved in smaller projects have the choice of a RIBA Concise PSC or a RIBA Domestic PSC. The domestic version is CRA 2015-compliant and reflects the different requirements of the CDM Regulations for domestic projects. It is essential that you use the current forms of contract.

Professional services contracts | 2

> **KEY FEATURES OF A RIBA PROFESSIONAL SERVICES CONTRACT**
>
> - Project Programme with key dates for all RIBA Plan of Work stages.
> - Schedule of Services setting out services at each RIBA Plan of Work stage.
> - Provision for setting numbers of meetings and detailing expenses.
> - Basic Fee plus fees for other services, with the choice of a lump sum, percentage or time charge.
> - Fee charging points – monthly invoicing linked to the Project Resources Programme is recommended (*not* linked to milestones, stage completion or any decision point beyond your control).
> - Provision for other consultants.
> - Principal Designer role (for domestic projects).
> - Each contract has clear guidance notes and a checklist.

Letter contracts

You may decide that the RIBA PSCs are not appropriate for all projects and that instead a simple letter contract is sufficient. Letter contracts have the advantage of being tailored to suit your normal practice and tend to be thought of as being more 'client friendly'. There are, however, a few points to note:

- The letter contract *must* comply with the requirements of RIBA Principle 2.2 and ARB Standard 4.4 (see text boxes above).
- The letter contract must include the project programme, with agreed start and completion dates.
- It is recommended that you invoice monthly in order to smooth your cash flow.
- Avoid linking invoicing and payment to milestones or outcomes beyond your control, for example, 'fee due on receipt of planning consent'. Also, client organisations with complex internal approval procedures (such as public bodies) may take considerable time in granting formal approval, even though the work has been completed. It can be difficult to expedite the process due to the approval structure in such cases.

Good Practice Guide: Fees

- Do not rely on references to other documents (such as a RIBA PSC). Unless included or attached to the letter contract, the RIBA PSCs' terms may not be considered contract documents. Worse still, they include options, which may be confusing for clients if they do not align with the letter contract.
- The letter contract must be up-to-date and take account of the CRA 2015 and obligations under the CDM Regulations.
- Remember that the letter contract is your business model and as such sets out the allocation of risks in terms of resourcing and time. You should therefore take legal advice on its wording; otherwise, it is recommended you use the RIBA PSCs.

Bespoke forms of contract

A letter contract with a client is one form of bespoke contract. However, bespoke contracts are commonly thought of as being prepared by the client (or their lawyers). The RIBA contracts have been developed with industry stakeholders and aim to be fair and balanced. However, some clients consider that the standard forms of contract skew the risk and liability towards them. Therefore they favour their own bespoke forms that are considered to rebalance specific risks and liabilities – potentially to their benefit.

Bespoke forms may be the only option when the RIBA PSCs do not apply; for example, when you are employed as an architect on non-traditional procurement routes. Developer clients acting as both client and contractor (such as housebuilders), design and build contractors and management contractors usually all require a specific set of services. Typically, they will have their own supplier contracts that suit their own business processes. One advantage of these types of project is that they are normally well-bounded – the scope of professional services and the project programme are more clearly defined than early stage, traditionally procured projects. Furthermore, they are usually lump sum contracts, where you as the architect take the design development and resourcing risks, usually to a clear programme.

Remember that all contracts (effectively subcontracts to construction contracts) are about allocation of risk: when working for a contractor, you are effectively a subcontractor. Therefore, be prepared to carefully consider the services you are providing, the resources necessary and the time required for delivery of the services. Contractors expect some negotiation and will be more commercially minded and dispassionate than consumer clients. It is therefore more important than ever that you generate a Project Resources Programme setting out the resourcing required over a total project timescale.

If a bespoke contract is presented by your client, it is recommended you seek legal advice and refer it to your professional indemnity insurer before agreeing to its terms because there is usually scope for negotiation.

> **KEY CONSIDERATIONS FOR BESPOKE CONTRACTS**
>
> - Consider the scope of your role, the number of stakeholders and the design team.
> - Aim to agree a schedule of monthly payments.
> - Do not agree to link fees to critical events beyond your control, for example, payment of fees on receipt of planning approval, approval of reserved matters or conditions or payment on receipt of approval by the client.
> - Prepare a Project Resources Programme.
> - Set out the deliverables, such as drawings and meetings.
> - Consider very carefully any contract clauses restricting variations to your services.
> - Take legal advice and/or check with your professional indemnity insurer.
> - Insert a termination clause dependent on payment and delivery.
> - Be prepared to negotiate.

Design and build procurement and novation agreements

The scope and type of services you provide on the design and build procurement route may vary considerably. Depending on your agreed role, you may remain on the client side throughout, with your role starting conventionally and then moving to an advisory role once the design and build contractor has been appointed. You may start on the client side and be novated to the contractor. You may work solely for the design and build contractor as their architect and have no direct involvement with the headline client. You may work for a developer client that controls the complete supply chain.

There is no strict definition of design and build procurement. You can find yourself supplying professional services at all or some of the RIBA Plan of Work stages. Bespoke forms of contract are prevalent due to this variety in industry practice. (The Construction Industry Council (CIC), though, has a standard CIC Novation Agreement.) In terms of fees, the same principle applies – the more 'well-bounded' the project and the better defined the tasks, the lower the resource and time risks are in terms of the services you provide (preferably accompanied by a responsibility matrix). For these reasons, working on the supply side with a developer or contractor can be an attractive option, and one that provides a degree of certainty in terms of tasks and outcomes lacking in traditional full services procurement. You may need to accept some risks though, particularly if you are involved in speculative contractor-side tendering. It follows that your fee should include a risk premium (as a starting point for negotiation, at least).

Letters of intent

A letter of intent can be used to confirm that both you and your client intend to create a contractual relationship for your services, prior to the final professional services contract documentation being issued for signature. In the case of commercial agreements, an intention to form a contract is assumed, unless clearly stated to the contrary, for example, by the insertion of 'subject to contract'. The letter may refer to contract documents and terms. A problem arises when the letter of intent is not followed by issuance of the contract itself, and both you and your client have to rely instead on the letter and on your conduct (i.e. carrying out your services and being paid for them). Under such circumstances (aside from any problems associated with liability), the scope of your services, when you are paid and how much will be unclear, unless set out in the letter.

Whether a letter of intent is a legally binding contract depends on the wording. Where there is a dispute about scope, the fees and performance will be decided by the courts. Commonly, each side will seek to interpret the letter to suit its own ends. Therefore, letters of intent create unforeseen risks due to the in-built uncertainty of the actual terms – even when sent in good faith. It is suggested they should be avoided.

CAUTIONARY TALE

A domestic client complained that the architect had invoiced for work that had not been agreed upon, and that they had never been sent a contract for his services.

The architect had sent a letter that made reference to a standard form of agreement for professional services that would be sent at a later date, but he failed to send it. It was found that: (a) the architect could not rely on a reference to the conditions of a standard form of contract because the client did not receive it and was therefore unaware of the terms; (b) the architect had failed to meet the standards required by the relevant codes of conduct, as the letter did not set out the requirements referred to in either RIBA Principle 2.2 or ARB Standard 4.4. In regard to fees, the letter set out neither the scope, nor the fee nor when payment was due. The architect received a reprimand and went unpaid.

Letters of comfort

A letter of comfort is distinct from a letter of intent. Its origin is in international banking, where complex, multi-party negotiations often take place. In the context of the construction industry, a letter of comfort sent from a client to an architect is intended to provide some reassurance that costs incurred as a result of complex negotiations – producing design information, for example – will be met, even though the exercise itself may be a wasted one. Such a letter of comfort is, however, unlikely to be interpreted as a contract and is in effect meaningless. It should not be relied upon as confirming that fees will be paid. If in doubt, take legal advice – or, better still, agree a lump sum or time-charge fee for your specific services at the outset. If this is refused, then at least you know and can review the amount of risk you are accepting – and any premium you may wish to try to include in the future.

Stuff happens: accommodating change in your contract

Throughout this chapter, the need to consider risks has been emphasised; that is, risks in relation to resource, time and the scope of your services. You will be agreeing a professional services contract and fees at an early stage when the levels of uncertainty are high. If you accept the risks, you should charge a premium for your services (as any contractor would). If you get the fee wrong or circumstances change (even with percentage fees), it may be impossible to recoup sufficient costs to break even. For obvious reasons, clients prefer lump sum fees, where the architect bears the financial risk. We discuss the different ways that you can charge for and limit exposure to risk in Chapter 4. Consider how you either accept, transfer or share these risks. Commercially, this is a typical part of negotiation and commercial clients may also ask you to accept extra work as part of your contract.

Because you are preparing the fee proposal at the point of greatest uncertainty, discuss risks with the client at the outset and aim to include terms that allow you to renegotiate or vary the fee if circumstances should change. Understandably, clients balk when they see all the fee risks passed back to them – after all, they want you to be primarily looking after their interests, not yours. The RIBA PSCs include standard clauses that pass the fee risks back to the client under a range of circumstances. This is one of the reasons why some clients dislike using standard forms of professional services contract.

Applying the principles of risk management, and in particular the principles that risk should sit with the party that can manage it best or that risks are shared, it becomes clear that architects should not be accepting risks beyond their control, such as changes to the scope that result in work that is additional to your basic services. Managing this effectively requires a discussion with the client about project risks and their effect on services. Such a discussion should take place at the outset and at regular points throughout the project. Invoicing monthly is an opportunity to provide a formal, short report on your fees in terms of planned and actual amounts. Relying on risk transfer clauses after the event can prove difficult, especially if you consider that the general long-term relationship with your client could be jeopardised.

Principal designer

If you provide services as principal designer (under the CDM Regulations), it is recommended that you treat these services as a separate appointment. The RIBA Principal Designer PSC is available for such an appointment. The RIBA Domestic PSC also includes a section on Principal Designer Services, setting out what is to be provided. The role is a statutory one and you ought only to agree to take it on if your practice is competent to carry it out effectively.

Summary

The contract with your client is one of the cornerstones of your business. It is a critical tool for managing your client's expectations regarding the services you will provide to achieve the project objectives. You should treat your contract with as much care and attention as the rest of the project. This preparatory work will frame the future relationship with your client.

Your contract must be in writing, clearly setting out the scope of your services and the payment terms. Using a standard professional services contract may be the most appropriate option. You may instead decide to issue a letter contract but, if you do, it must comply with the minimum requirements of the profession. If you are providing partial services, make sure that the exact scope is clearly defined. Be alert to the dangers of using a letter of intent and make sure that it is followed as soon as possible by a full professional services contract for the project. Getting the contract right – at the outset – is essential. You should use it as a primary reference point: when the scope is clearly stated and agreed with the client before you start work, it will be easier to manage change as the project progresses.

Professional services contracts

> **WATCH POINTS**
>
> - Consider your professional services contract as a separate project with four stages: pre-contract, contract, contract performance and post-contract.
> - Carry out a pre-contract preliminary assessment. Formally evaluate the project characteristics in terms of fluidity, risk, uncertainty, complexity, number of stakeholders and procurement route.
> - Consider the effects these characteristics have on the scope of services, resources required and time.
> - Prepare a Project Resources Programme – resource over time against RIBA Plan of Work stage activities.
> - Discuss with your client the project characteristics and the allocation of risk, using the contract to manage the relationship.
> - Consider what is required for domestic clients under the Consumer Rights Act 2015, where relevant.
> - Continuously monitor and evaluate change in scope, outputs and progress against the Project Resources Programme.

Endnotes

1. RIBA, *Code of Professional Conduct* (London: RIBA, 2019). Available at: www.architecture.com/knowledge-and-resources/resources-landing-page/code-of-professional-conduct [17 August 2020].
2. ARB, *Architects Code: Standards of Professional Conduct and Practice* (London: ARB, 2017). Available at: https://arb.org.uk/architect-information/architects-code-standards-of-conduct-and-practice [17 August 2020].
3. Details on and sample copies of the RIBA Professional Services Contracts are available from www.architecture.com/riba-contracts.

3

Office finances and charge out rates

This chapter looks at how office finances affect fees and charge out rates. It is important to understand the key variables and how they impact on the cost of office resources in order to be confident about your charge out rates. In a competitive market, it is also instructive to compare how your office is doing with other practices by using benchmarking data. This chapter aims to:

- show how benchmarking data can be used
- explain how to use office financial data
- provide a method for calculating your charge out rate
- explore profit and the impact of risk
- show how to take account of non-productive time.

Benchmarking and published data

A range of benchmarking information is available to practitioners, including published information in the *Architects' Journal* and the RIBA data available to RIBA Chartered Practices. This information allows for comparison against variables such as practice size, profitability and income per fee earner or revenue by practice size, as well as charge out rates. By comparing your practice against similar firms and sectors, it is possible to gauge the relative performance of your business. The following examples are taken from the RIBA Business Benchmarking survey 2018.[1]

Revenue benchmarking

Revenue benchmarking can be expressed as an average mean practice revenue for a particular practice size (Figure 3.1) or average mean practice revenue per head for different practice sizes (Figure 3.2). For smaller practices of up to 10 people, there is a revenue range of approximately £50,000 to £60,000 for each fee-earning member of staff.

Profit benchmarking

The RIBA benchmarking survey considers revenue; however, the survey does state that 'profits will typically include a substantial element of the pay received by the partners, directors or sole principals'. This makes it difficult to differentiate salaries from profit. Figure 3.3 expresses profit as an average amount based on practice size.

The majority of RIBA Chartered Practices (73%) in the United Kingdom are limited companies. There can be a tax advantage in paying directors a lower salary while awarding them a larger dividend (i.e. share of the profit).

Benchmarking charge out rates

The RIBA benchmarking survey data for average hourly rates used to calculate fees records a wide range of charge out rates, with partners and directors

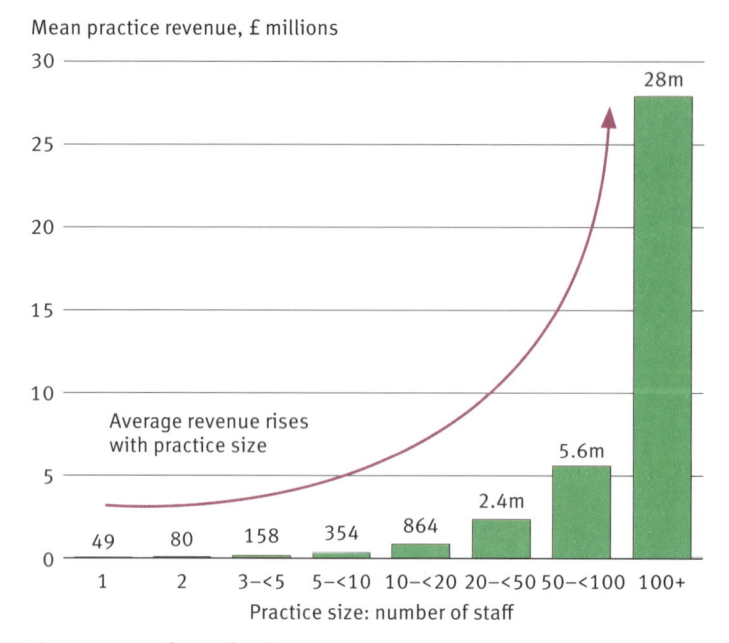

Figure 3.1: Average revenue by practice size

Office finances and charge out rates 3

Mean practice revenue per head, £000s

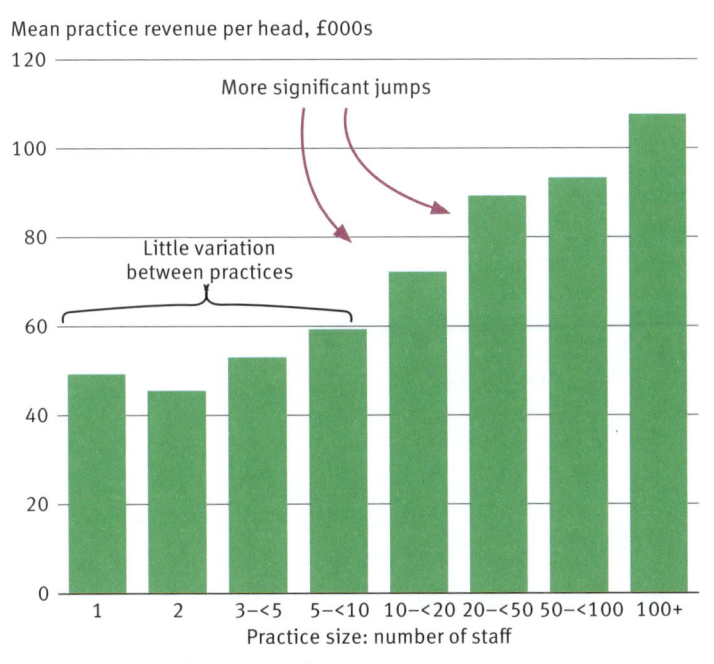

More significant jumps

Little variation between practices

Practice size: number of staff: 1, 2, 3–<5, 5–<10, 10–<20, 20–<50, 50–<100, 100+

Figure 3.2: Average revenue for fee-earning staff

Average (mean) profits, £000

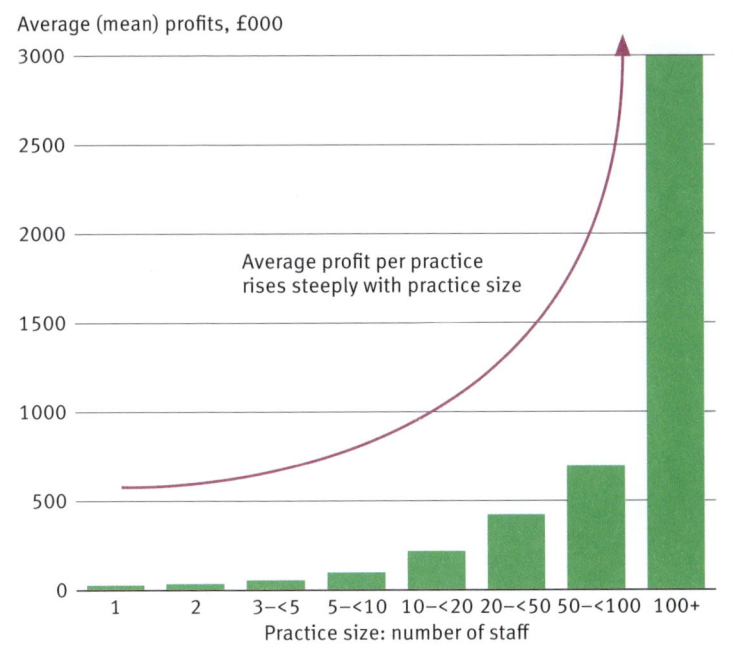

Average profit per practice rises steeply with practice size

Practice size: number of staff: 1, 2, 3–<5, 5–<10, 10–<20, 20–<50, 50–<100, 100+

Figure 3.3: Average profit for different sizes of practice

Good Practice Guide: Fees

Figure 3.4: Average hourly charge out rates used to calculate fees

Role	Hourly rate £ (approx.)
Partners/directors/sole principals	105
Salaried partners/directors	120
Associates	95
Architects 5+ years	80
Architects <5 years	75
Technologists	65
Arch. assistants (Part 2)	60
Arch. assistants (Part 1)	50
Other chartered	70
Other fee-earning	55
Office management / support & admin	20

Note: Average hourly rates refer to the charge out rates used by practices for calculating fees on projects, and are not necessarily the rates directly charged to clients.

charging over twice the rate quoted for less experienced staff. There is a clustering of rates among architects with five or more years' experience (Figure 3.4).

Charge out rates should not only reflect level of experience, but also the type of commission, the level of risk and value to the client of the work being undertaken. While benchmarking helps by providing some comparison with other practices, the individual profile of a commission will make a difference to the charge out rate quoted to a client. It is for this reason that it is vital you know the break-even point for a given level of staff.

There is also a difference between (1) the general staff hourly rate used to calculate fees within the office and (2) the charge out rate quoted to a client to undertake a specific commission paid at an hourly rate. The latter is a commercial decision based upon what the market will stand, given the nature of the professional service being offered.

The charge out rates for the different sizes of practice set out in Table 3.1 show that it is possible for smaller practices to compete with larger firms on fees.

3 Office finances and charge out rates

Table 3.1: Average charge out rates by practice size: £ per hour (2018)

	Practice size									
	1	2	3–<5	5–<10	10–<20	20–<50	50–<100	100+	ALL	2017 ALL
Equity partners, shareholder directors or sole principals	77	80	92	100	121	130	199	146	104	101
Salaried partners or non-shareholder directors	n/a	n/a	n/a	100	95	115	164	168	120	106
Associate directors or associates	n/a	n/a	66	86	93	94	121	112	92	88
Architects (5+ years ARB registered)	n/a	n/a	71	82	84	82	93	88	81	80
Architects (<5 years ARB registered)	n/a	n/a	69	73	74	79	79	75	74	73
Technologists	n/a	n/a	54	61	67	60	78	67	63	60
Architectural assistants (Part 2)	n/a	n/a	53	60	62	59	66	60	60	58
Architectural assistants (Part 1)	n/a	n/a	46	51	50	48	57	49	50	48
Other chartered construction professionals	n/a	n/a	n/a	n/a	83	57	n/a	n/a	67	61
Other fee-earning staff	n/a	n/a	49	49	49	51	57	65	52	53
Office management/support and admin	n/a	20	14	19	17	15	27	20	18	16

Benchmarking percentage fees

There are a number of surveys available that cover percentage fees charged for both new build and refurbishment projects across a variety of procurement routes. These do not, however, always reflect the wide variation that exists in fees. Organisations putting competitive fee bids out for tender sometimes provide anonymised feedback to unsuccessful candidates detailing the range of fees quoted. In such cases, percentage fees can be far lower than the average in the benchmarking data illustrated here.

Benchmarking summary

Benchmarking data is worthwhile and a reminder that there is no one-size-fits-all solution to practice finances. What is important is to understand your own organisation and how your hourly rate is calculated. You can then make an informed judgment on the appropriate fee to charge for a defined level of service.

Calculating a charge out rate

There are several ways to calculate a charge out rate. Methods include using:

- a factor of salary
- a factor of whole office costs
- net employee costs plus a percentage.

Whatever system is chosen, risk must be a consideration. This can either be shared with the client, transferred or added to the fee.

The most reliable method involves using your own office's financial data. If you have been running your practice for several years and have management accounts, gathering the information necessary is relatively straightforward.

To work out a charge out rate you need to establish the cost to the office of having a fee-earning member of staff at their workstation for an entire year. Include all overheads, then convert this cost into an hourly rate. There are three components to this calculation:

1. total turnover or revenue of the practice over a year
2. cost of overheads for that year, including the cost of any non-fee-earning support staff
3. profit for the year (excluding salaries).

Office finances and charge out rates 3

If you are a newly formed practice, calculate your outgoings, including all overheads, based upon your anticipated workflow and revenue – and target an appropriate profit or surplus for the year.

Calculating a charge out rate

IN PRACTICE EXAMPLE

Consider a small practice comprising two principals and four fee-earning members of staff.

Assume that the practice is outside central London and therefore has comparatively low overheads with, perhaps, one part-time administrative support staff member. The practice has an annual revenue of £500,000, with overheads of £125,000 and architectural/technical staff costs – including principals – of £275,000. This yields a profit, or surplus, of £100,000 (see Figure 3.5).

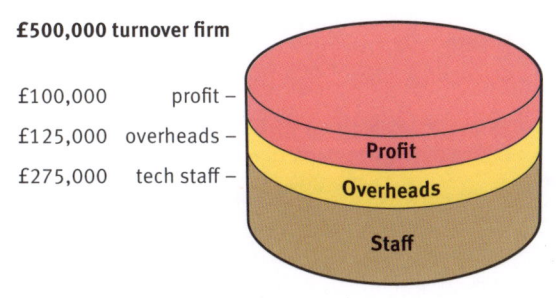

£500,000 turnover firm

£100,000   profit –
£125,000   overheads –
£275,000   tech staff –

Figure 3.5: The office cake

In order to calculate a charge out rate, it is necessary to first take away the profit and consider only the net turnover, or outgoings, inclusive of staff costs and overheads (see Figure 3.6).

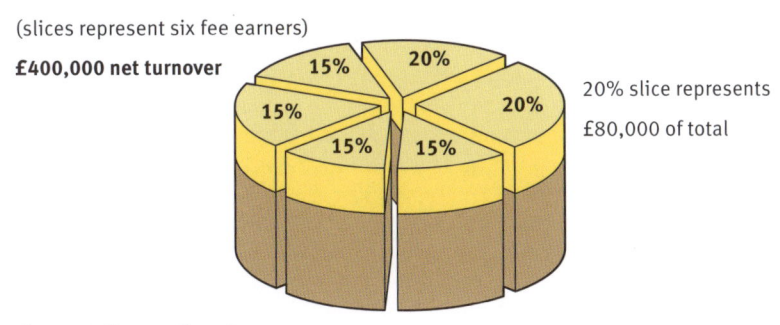

(slices represent six fee earners)

£400,000 net turnover

20% slice represents £80,000 of total

Figure 3.6: The net office cake

37

Apportion a slice of the office cake to each member of the fee-earning staff according to their salary or annual cost to the office. In the case of Figure 3.6, there are six fee-earning members of staff whose cost to the office is roughly equal.

In order to arrive at an hourly charge out rate, divide each slice of the office cake by the number of working days in a year. Assume, for example, 227 working days (although this may vary, depending upon the firm and holiday entitlement, and does not account for sickness). The resulting figure is the cost per day. Divide it by the number of working hours in a day (say 7.5 hours) to get the hourly rate. In Figure 3.6, the most senior member of staff represents 20% of the total, therefore the calculation works as follows:

- total office net cake = £400,000
- one slice = 20% of the total cake (i.e. £80,000 is the net cost to the office of employing a senior member of staff for a whole year inclusive of overheads)
- divide £80,000 by 227 days = £352 per day (net cost to the office)
- divide by 7.5 hours = £47 per hour (net cost to the office).

It should, however, be noted that this rate assumes that the staff member is fee earning 100% of the time and makes no allowance for profit or risk.

In order to arrive at a charge out rate, first add a percentage for non-productive time, appropriate to the person's role in the office. For a junior member of technical staff, you might assume 95% productivity, allowing, on average, half a day a week for training, research, non-project related admin and sickness. However, for a senior member of staff, who may be involved in marketing, meeting clients, carrying out unpaid feasibility studies, it could be much lower. If the practice keeps timesheets, it ought to be possible to put definition into this 'chargeable hours' percentage. Assuming 60% productivity for the most senior member of staff pushes up the net cost rate of £47 per hour to a break-even point of £78 per hour.

In order to arrive at a charge out rate, it is necessary to then add a percentage for profit. This can vary enormously, depending upon the size of the practice, competition, market value and the sector in which the practice is working. The RIBA Business Benchmarking data shows a range of between 10% and 50%. If 25% were to be applied, the charge out rate would increase from the £78 break-even point to a £101 per hour charge out rate.

Note: Accountants calculate profit as a percentage of revenue cost, so, for example, a practice wanting to make a 20% profit will need to mark up their costs by 25%.

The example above shows how to calculate a charge out rate for a senior member of staff. The same approach can be used to calculate the charge out rate for every member of staff, based on their cost to the office and therefore proportion – or slice – of office 'cake', that is, turnover.

Finally, there may be risk associated with a specific commission that warrants a higher charge out rate. The professional service you are providing may be of a highly specialised nature and therefore have a higher value. This is a commercial decision determined by what the market will stand.

Other methods of calculating a charge out rate

The example provided is just one of the ways of calculating a charge out rate and applies to sole practitioners, micro and small practices. Medium and large practices will almost certainly have their own system for generating charge out rates based upon agreed profit margins. There are, however, several other models which have been used successfully over many years. The RIBA Fee Calculator also helps practices prepare resource-based fee calculations, tailored to their practice, projects and clients.

Historical data

Using historical data built up by your practice over the years is the most reliable way of arriving at a charge out rate, particularly when the firm is well established. However, relying solely on these rates in isolation can sometimes make a practice uncompetitive or, alternatively, result in it charging below the market rate.

As a factor of staff salary

Charge out rates can be calculated as a factor of staff salary, ranging from two times through to four times the net hourly cost of employing the member of staff concerned. If this system has been used successfully by a practice over a number of years, it makes good sense to continue using the practice's historical data. Some practices prefer to apply a uniform charge out rate across all employees. This makes calculating the fee simpler. Another accounting strategy is to treat the partners or directors of the practice as an overhead and not to assign their cost to specific projects. This approach, of course, increases the charge out rates for individual staff members in order to cover the resultant higher overheads.

Whatever system is adopted, it is important to be confident about the figures being used. This curbs the natural temptation to cut fees in order to win work.

Good Practice Guide: Fees

> **CAUTIONARY TALE**
>
> An experienced sole practitioner with an excellent track record of designing one-off houses and good local knowledge was approached by a prospective client. The architect spent time listening to their requirements, visited the site and gave a detailed fee breakdown and service proposal, providing a full explanation of how his service worked.
>
> The fee had been calculated by working out the task needed, taking into account break-even point, profit and risk. Having received the fee proposal, the client later came back to the architect, explaining that they had received another quote and asked whether they would like to review the fee. The architect politely responded that they had reviewed the fee, the professional training they had received, and the expert local knowledge they brought to the project, and on this basis declined to revise the fee.
>
> In this example, the architect was confident that the fee quoted was right for the job. The fee had been calculated in a methodical manner and they knew the value of their service.

The scenario described in the cautionary tale may be familiar to some architects, particularly sole practitioners who deal with domestic clients. The postscript is that the architect concerned was, in fact, appointed on the basis of the original fee. It is therefore both a cautionary tale for any client trying to devalue an architect's work and a positive lesson for any architect on the importance of being confident about how you arrived at your fee.

Summary

A charge out rate ought to be the basis of every fee proposal. It links the hours required to carry out the commission to the total fee to be charged. Understanding your break-even point allows you to underpin the way your fees are built up. Chapter 6 covers monitoring and change control and explains the importance of having a rational plan in making it easier to build a case for additional fees when the scope or brief changes.

Office finances and charge out rates 3

> **WATCH POINTS**
>
> - Understand your organisation and how its finances work.
> - Calculate your break-even point and then build up your charge out rate, taking account of profit and risk.
> - Review your staff talent and establish an appropriate percentage for non-productive time.
> - Recognise the limitations of benchmarking data.
> - Understand your own sector and the competition when making an allowance for profit.

Endnotes

1   RIBA. *RIBA Business Benchmarking 2018* (London: RIBA, 2018).

4

Fee calculation and negotiation: how to put together an effective fee proposal

This chapter discusses how to calculate the fee for a project so that it reflects accurately the resources necessary to deliver the outputs required by an estimated programme. It considers how to take account of project risks – and the value you contribute – at the different stages of a project. It takes the same project approach applied in Chapter 2, where the professional services contract is regarded as a project in itself, having a beginning (resources), a middle (programme) and an end (outputs). Chapter 3 discussed how to calculate costs. Data from your own practice will give you the greatest degree of confidence in your hourly, daily and other related costs, but may also be part of the problem. Agreeing an inadequate fee may mean you will not recover sufficient costs to make the practice sustainable or are not managing time effectively. This chapter builds on the idea that time is your only true resource. It explores:

- different methods of charging and their significance
- subconsultants and how to charge for them
- how to build up a detailed fee proposal by linking outputs, resources and time
- fee bidding and negotiation
- partial services
- entering new sectors.

Fees and expenses

There are three main methods of charging for your services:

- lump sum or sums
- specified percentage or percentages applied to the construction cost
- time charge or charges.

These three methods are designed to reflect the different risks concerning resource and payment agreed by the parties. All three are an option in the standard forms and may appear to be similar. They do, however, differ in the allocation and ownership of both the resource and time risks expressed in your fees (as well as, possibly, future liabilities). Consider the time, resources and accepted risks, remembering that risk transfer often warrants a premium being added to the fee. In practice, the contract for your professional services may comprise a combination of these methods, depending on the allocation of risk.

Lump sum – a fixed fee

A lump sum contract is one where, in principle, the fee fixed for the services set out in the contract cannot be varied. This type of contract is attractive to clients because it gives cost certainty at an early stage in the project. For example, if the scope of services includes RIBA Plan of Work Stage 3, you as the architect are effectively taking all the resource and time risks associated with the development of the design. Despite this, clients may still be concerned that they are overpaying or paying a premium.

CAUTIONARY TALE

A new, ambitious practice was appointed by a developer client for the speculative refurbishment of a small office building. The client had an absolute, finite project budget and, in order to obtain a return on their investment, a fixed project programme. Planning consent was not required. The project was to follow a design and build procurement route, with full services up to Stage 5, whereupon the architect and the team would be novated to the contractor. A fixed lump sum for the architect's professional services was agreed in a straightforward bespoke contract drafted by the client. What could go wrong?

Nothing – at least as far as the client was concerned. Following the signing of the agreement, the developer client was approached by a prospective tenant who agreed to take the whole building. The project

> budget doubled, design development was extended to accommodate the new tenant (in effect, another stakeholder, i.e. an indirect client), and procurement changed into a hybrid form that involved extensive involvement by the architect at Stage 5. The architect took specialist legal advice. It was concluded that the wording of the lump sum contract was such that there was no scope to vary the terms. Terminating the contract unilaterally would be a breach of contract and the architect could be sued for a failure in performance. Putting the practice into administration was considered, but eventually they agreed to take a significant loss, which they had to borrow against and which set back future growth. None of the changes that took place were envisaged by client at the time the contract was formed.

If a lump sum fee is agreed, set clear boundaries around the scope of services. It is strongly advised that you qualify your fee proposal by stating that, should the scope or programme vary significantly, you have the option of renegotiating the fee to reflect these changes. Due to the fixed nature of a lump sum fee, it is important that it is agreed at the outset that the fee can be varied should the scope of services change – thereby, effectively sharing some of the risks with the client.

Percentage fee

Conventionally, a percentage fee is based on the final construction cost. It is simple to calculate and most appropriate for traditional procurement, where the architect is working on every RIBA Plan of Work stage. However, the final cost of your professional services to the client is not known until the project is completed. It takes no account of the true resource costs or the total project timescale, as there is no direct link between the fee and the resources required to carry out the works. It also lacks transparency. There is a longstanding – but misplaced – suspicion that a percentage fee incentivises the design team to allow project costs to rise. Furthermore, the percentage method locks clients into paying fees that may not represent accurately the true costs. For example, the architect's fee is linked to construction market costs and these may increase or decrease independently of professional resource costs. This may, in turn, also create cost and time risks for the architect.

Complications can also arise when projects come to involve more design development than anticipated or post-tender value engineering is required. This is, in effect, where the time you spend is not reflected in the out-turn total construction costs, due to the disconnect between your costs (time spent) and the method of charging for your services (the percentage fee). You may on occasion be providing services at particular RIBA Plan of Work stages that involve a percentage of a percentage. The RIBA Professional Services Contracts provide for this, and it is also accounted for in some bespoke forms of contract.

Even when working to a percentage fee, you should still prepare a detailed Project Resources Programme for the whole project. Delays may occur in the programme for reasons beyond your control, such as delays in client decision-making, planning delays or delays in the construction programme. You need to be able to monitor the effect of such delays against your Project Resources Programme. Although the cost risk rests with the client, there is no direct connection between the architect's resource costs and the fee charged, or transparency when services and timescales change. This, in turn, creates cost and time risks for the architect; for example, tenders may happen to come in lower than expected.

> **CAUTIONARY TALE**
>
> An architect agreed a professional services contract that was based on a percentage of the total construction cost. Due to considerable delays outside the client's control, the project proceeded very slowly and over-ran by 12 months; however, the percentage fee remained the same. Delay does not necessarily reduce resourcing pro rata and the architect's costs increased.

Time charge

A time charge is based on the actual time spent, calculated according to a previously agreed hourly or daily rate or else a set of rates dependent on the qualifications and seniority of the staff employed. It is an appropriate method of charging when the boundaries of your services cannot be defined; for example, where the project is still being investigated at Stage 0. It is also appropriate when additional services are not directly linked to RIBA Plan of Work stages or are purely advisory and, in effect, on demand. Even when the scope is defined, the cost risk associated with your fee remains with the client. The final cost to the client is not known until the service is completed.

Most clients want some reassurance that fees will not escalate and therefore ask for a fee ceiling. This should be reviewed regularly and at each stage. If the client agrees to a time charge fee, it should not then be seen as risk-free. You need to be able to account for every hour you spend and the service provided.

It is important to keep comprehensive records of time spent, recording exactly what was done at each RIBA Plan of Work stage. This can increase the

Fee calculation and negotiation: how to put together an effective fee proposal 4

pressure on you, as it focuses on the value each hour spent adds to the project, especially at the early stages. You must regularly review your time and be prepared to discount or adjust your fee, if necessary. Invoice regularly and be prepared to explain how and why time has been spent – especially if the fee account is queried. Not doing so can lead to a dispute.

Expenses

Consider expenses as part of the total fee and subject to negotiation. To that effect, you may add a lump sum, include expenses in the fee (in both instances, taking any cost risk), add a percentage to the fee or charge the net cost plus a handling charge. Again, it is important to keep comprehensive records. Any handling charge needs to be transparent and stated at the outset. If you include expenses in the fee, and therefore the risk, it is important to be confident that they are based on similar projects and reasonable.

Combining methods

It is not unusual to combine two of these methods of charging. A key point to consider is that, particularly in traditional procurement, you will be preparing the fee proposal at the time in the project when there is the greatest uncertainty or fluidity. In view of this lack of certainty, the allocation of risk is not necessarily straightforward. Suggesting certain steps is one way of reducing the risks to both you and the client, starting with a feasibility study. Carefully consider all factors. For example, repeat work for a client reduces risks, whereas a new client in a new sector can represent a leap into the unknown. It may therefore be prudent to use a combination of methods, depending on your assessment of the project risk. The more thorough and formal this assessment, the greater the certainty. By building up records of your assessment, you also build points of reference for the future.

The method of charging set against the perceived levels of uncertainty and associated risks can be set out in a simple chart (Table 4.1). The core aim is to make evident the link between risk and the method of charging. Included is the perceived value you add, as this may have an influence on how and what you charge. This chart is not intended to be prescriptive – but the simple method of analysis should help make you aware when you are accepting project risks. For example, Stage 5 is relatively high-risk because you have no control over the construction programme, nor some of the difficulties that could be encountered. You may decide to accept the effect that contractor performance has on your resources, and make allowance for it in a lump sum fee for this stage.

Table 4.1: Project risks, value and methods of charging

RIBA Plan of Work stage	Estimated uncertainty	Risk assessment	Value of your services at each stage	Appropriate method of charging
0 – Strategic Definition	Fluid: high uncertainty	High risk	HIGH	Time charge
1 – Preparation and Briefing	Defining boundaries: high uncertainty	High risk – but familiarity with process	HIGH–MEDIUM	Time charge/lump sum
2 – Concept Design	Potential control through the brief: well-bounded but potentially high levels of uncertainty due to client changes	High–medium risk	HIGH	Time charge/lump sum
3 – Spatial Coordination	Well-bounded	Low risk	HIGH – especially in planning applications	Lump sum
4 – Technical Design	Well-bounded	Low risk	MEDIUM	Lump sum
5 – Manufacturing and Construction	The architect has no control over the duration of the final construction programme	High risk: a delay to the construction programme will have a direct effect on your resourcing	MEDIUM–LOW	Time charge: contract administration *or* Lump sum linked to the contract programme *or* A combination of time charge and lump sum
6 – Handover	Consider defects	Medium risk	MEDIUM	Time charge
7 – Use	Optional: you can agree the scope separately as a 'defined service' with outcomes or as a time charge cost per visit	Medium risk (Beware of unforeseen events – such as latent defects, which may be very time consuming)	MEDIUM, potentially HIGH	Time charge
	Post-occupancy evaluation: can be a lump sum	Low risk – if well-bounded		Lump sum

Fee calculation and negotiation: how to put together an effective fee proposal

Consultants and subconsultants

In traditional procurement, where the architect provides the full range of services, the architect usually advises the client about other design team appointments required to carry out the project. This is reflected in the RIBA Professional Services Contracts, which provide for the architect to: give relevant advice to the client regarding the appointment of other consultants at Stage 1; coordinate information from the client's consultants at Stages 2 to 5; and liaise with consultants on the making good of defects at Stage 6. The RIBA contract wording is important: it restricts your service to 'Advise on the Other Client Appointments required' and 'Coordinate the relevant information received from the Other Client Appointments'. This may not reflect accurately the activity and amount of time that goes into managing the consultants in a design team.

When working directly for a developer-contractor providing specific services, you may still be called upon to coordinate information from other consultants in the project team.

Increasingly, clients require architects to appoint some or all of the design team consultants as *subconsultants* to be employed by the architect, rather than the client appointing them direct. The value of this to the client is twofold: they have a single point of contact contractually and a single point of design liability.

Subconsultancy, however, adds to the risk for the architect by making you liable for design services beyond your professional competence. Therefore, it is important you obtain agreement from your professional indemnity insurer, as this is liable to raise your premium. Any additional premium must be maintained to the limit of your agreed liability. Your commitment to additional costs will therefore extend far beyond the completion of the project. (Additional liability may be offset by collateral warranty agreements.) In addition to higher insurance costs, you should also allow a sum for the management of subconsultants (typically, 10–15% of the subconsultants' fees). The RIBA, recognising that subconsultancy is increasingly required, publishes the RIBA Subconsultant Professional Services Contract for use when contracting with subconsultants or when the architect is appointed as a subconsultant.

More immediately, you will be responsible for paying and managing your subconsultants. Their non-performance is now your non-performance. This includes ensuring the delivery and coordination of information.

Although subconsultancy is now part of normal project delivery, it is important to recognise that the administrative and liability burden this puts on small and sole practitioners is proportionally far higher than it is for medium-sized and large practices. Small practitioners do not have access to the same level of administrative support or financial resources as a medium-sized practice. It is simply not part of their business model.

The sole practitioner becomes, in effect, a small, multi-disciplinary practice for that project only. As well as the additional risk and liability, there is an increase in the time devoted to managing the appointments and the team. All this needs to be factored into your fee proposal. This includes adding a premium for accepting the risk, as well as the administrative costs in connection with your time spent administering the team, rather than just coordinating consultant information, which would be the usual service.

It is worth noting that the additional work, cost and risk need to be weighed against the benefits to the client. A prudent approach is to first discuss your increased liabilities with the potential client, particularly the disproportionate effect on your practice. For example, the single point of liability has effectively resulted in additional insurance premium costs; so too, the consultant's professional indemnity taken out as additional cover. That cost has to be carried either by the architect or the client, maintained for a minimum of six years. Although the single point of liability is potentially attractive to a client, the potential benefit will necessarily be offset by additional costs.

Identifying and communicating value

Architects add value to all the projects they work on. The scale of that value, though, varies, depending on the RIBA Plan of Work stage and the services provided. The value brought to any project is a direct result of talent, design education and training, professional skills built up over time and practice or sector experience. Architects continually update their skills through CPD and may also gain additional expertise over and above the normal professional standards of architectural practice, for example, in the conservation of historic buildings. While these skills and expertise may be advertised on your website and through social media, you must ensure they are also reflected in the fee you charge for your professional services. Some services are of greater value than others. For example, carrying out visual inspections for defects at Stage 6 is time-consuming, routine specialist work, but of relatively low value to the project as a whole. In contrast, developing a design that meets complex planning requirements is of high value and the success of a project depends on it.

Differential rates reflecting value

In a medium-sized or large practice, different staff will be 'charged in' to a project proposal or 'charged out' to clients at differential rates, depending on skills, role and experience. This option is not ordinarily available to a sole practitioner or micro-practice. However, some services are clearly of more value than others. Once you have calculated your break-even point, consider the value you bring to each particular stage, as well as the risk and profit.

One way to objectivise your assessment of value is through *substitution*: who else could carry out this work and what qualifications would they need?

As a rule of thumb, most value added comes at the early RIBA Plan of Work stages, when an architect offers their professional insight into the brief and deploys their creative skills. At later stages, greater value is added through an understanding and experience of the regulatory systems affecting development and management of health and safety.

Adding extra value

Successful fee proposals often offer above what is initially requested. In a competitive environment, adding extra value will distinguish your proposal from others. Use the fee proposal as an opportunity to see where extra value can be extracted from a site which would more than offset a higher initial fee. In the context of an end-user, indicate that you can offer solutions for extracting further value from the project. For example, additional facilities or the skills and experience to achieve, or even exceed, sustainability targets and reduce cost-in-use (where the value you bring more than compensates for the higher fees). It is crucial that you appreciate the value you add and how it can be monetised when it exceeds the mutual benefit of a normal fee proposal.

Building up a full services fee proposal: it's all about time

This method treats the fee proposal as a separate project and builds a fee proposal using *time*, *resource required* and *outputs* over an estimated Project Resources Programme. For completeness, it is assumed you are preparing a fee proposal for a full services commission using traditional procurement, where the architect's services are required across the RIBA Plan of Work Stages 1 to 6. You can then use the method for particular stages or specific tasks.

The early stages of a project are the riskiest due to the greater potential unknowns. The better defined or bounded the project, the fewer the unknowns. Be prepared to plan for alternative scenarios by recalibrating the four variables: time, resource required, outputs and Project Resources Programme.

Remember that this is both your business model and the basis for communicating with the client. In principle, introducing some certainty or fixity at this critical stage can reduce risk and set the parameters for unforeseen changes as the project develops. Consider it a live method that you monitor and review regularly and adapt to suit changes as they occur.

1. Prepare an outline Project Resources Programme

Sketch out an outline Project Resources Programme that covers all the Stages (as demonstrated using a simple example in Figure 4.1). Stages 1 to 6 are traditionally where architects devote most of their time. You may decide to omit Stage 0, but include an allowance for Stage 7 – it is not part of your fee proposal, but monitoring the performance of a building in use against the design predictions will inform future designs and build up a database of projects.

2. Identify risk activities

Activities that can be controlled in terms of resource, time and output are generally low risk. For example, Stage 2 Concept Design is broadly under your control. Activities beyond your control, which rely on the performance of others, can be medium to high risk. For example, Stage 5 Manufacturing and Construction is dependent on contractor performance. The time spent on pre-application planning advice and dealing with the planning application(s) also needs to include a realistic assessment of factors beyond your control.

3. Include meeting points for each stage

Include an allowance for regular project review meetings with the client, as well as meetings at specific stages. Allow for regular meetings with the design team and with the local authority. Include regular construction progress meetings at Stage 5.

4. List outputs across the Project Resources Programme

Outputs include: the project brief, feasibility studies, responsibility matrices, concept design, detailed design studies, outline specifications, planning application, final specifications, drawing packages, manufacturing/construction information, health and safety/fire safety information, Building Regulations application, tender information, project reports, manuals and defects reports.

5. Allocate resource to each activity and output

Estimate the time in days required to complete each activity and prepare outputs.

6. Estimate your project break-even point cost

Using your break-even point calculations, calculate the cost of each RIBA Plan of Work stage and build up a total cost for the estimated Project Resources

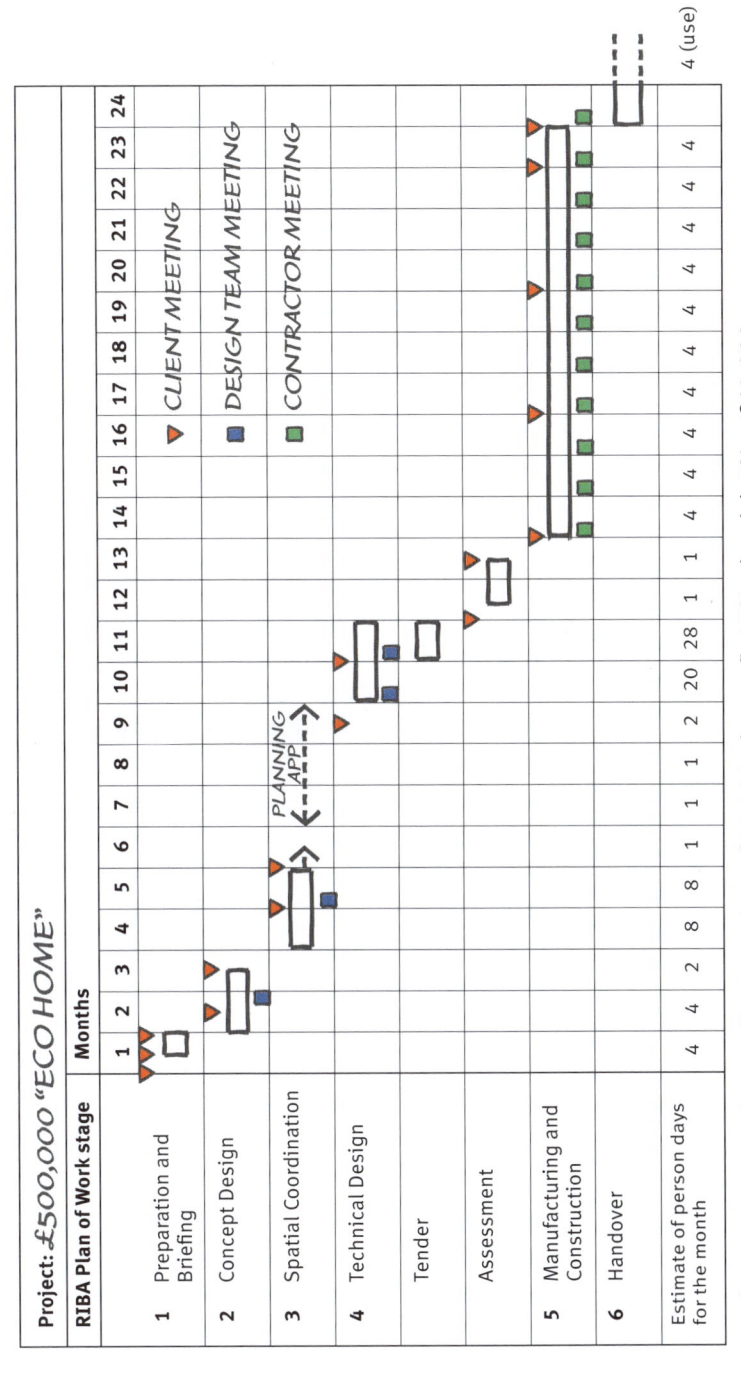

4 Fee calculation and negotiation: how to put together an effective fee proposal

Project: £500,000 "ECO HOME"

RIBA Plan of Work stage	Months																								
	1	2	3	4	5	6	7	8	9	10	11	12	13	14	15	16	17	18	19	20	21	22	23	24	
1 Preparation and Briefing																									
2 Concept Design																									
3 Spatial Coordination																									
4 Technical Design																									
Tender																									
Assessment																									
5 Manufacturing and Construction																									
6 Handover																									
Estimate of person days for the month	4	4	2	8	8	1	1	1	2	20	28	1	1	4	4	4	4	4	4	4	4	4	4	4	4 (use)

Markers shown: ▼ CLIENT MEETING · ■ DESIGN TEAM MEETING · ■ CONTRACTOR MEETING · PLANNING APP

Total 125 person days @ £400 per day = £50,000 *plus* profit 15% *plus* risk 5% = £60,000

Figure 4.1: Example Project Resources Programme

Programme. You now have a reasonable estimate of the cost to you based on the four variables: time, resource required, outputs and Project Resources Programme. Proposing or agreeing to a fee below this total break-even point cost will mean you have forecast losing money – unless, that is, you alter one or more variables to reduce the resource allocated.

7. Make a first fee estimate

Using the break-even point costs, add a percentage for profit to reinvest in the practice to give you a second 'baseline' fee.

8. Make a second fee estimate that includes allowances for accepted risks, added value and profit

The aim is to estimate the premium value of any risks you are asked to accept, and to identify areas where the added value is significant, possibly by varying the resource rate for particular stages. Finally, add a broad percentage for the profit required to maintain the investment necessary to sustain your practice.[1]

9. Reality check

The resultant fee option may be higher than the current market rate. For a simple reality check, convert the estimated fee into a percentage of the estimated construction cost and compare it with the broad benchmark data for that type of work. Note, though, that the benchmarking data is generalised and may not accurately reflect your type of work, nor the area in which you practise.

10. Iterate – then iterate again

You can use your initial estimate to carry out a number of fairly basic iterations, making alterations to a different variable each time. For example, the estimated Project Resources Programme may be too long. However, experience from previous projects should give you a reliable indication of what to expect. Do not be tempted to be unrealistic.

11. Subconsultants and expenses

If you have agreed to employ one or more subconsultants, ensure that you have included any additional professional indemnity premium(s) plus a charge for management and administration. This can be charged as a separate fee or included in the total fee.

If you have agreed that statutory fees are to be included, ensure they are confirmed in advance and charged as a separate item.

If it has been agreed that project expenses are to be included, include either a lump sum or an estimate subject to change, based on data from previous projects.

12. Fine-tune and play back

Prepare a final draft fee proposal to include: the project fee(s) (including an allowance for risk, value and profit), statutory costs, subconsultant costs (if required), expenses (if required) and a summary of the Project Resources Programme, based on the RIBA Plan of Work stage headings, with the agreed start date and an estimate of the finish date.

(Do *not* include your scenario options and sketch programmes – these can be referred to later on in negotiation, if required.)

Specify any exclusions, for example, consultant fees, statutory costs and expenses (if you have agreed not to include these). Invoicing points are discussed in Chapter 7.

Review the final draft and try to be objective in your assessment. If possible, share the proposal with a colleague (but not a competitor).

In following this approach, it is likely to conclude with you submitting a proposal that comprises a combination of: lump sum(s), time charge(s) and/or percentage, especially in respect of risks beyond your control. Many practitioners consider it beneficial to agree a set of lump sums for the earlier RIBA Plan of Work stages (where the architect has greater control, lower risk and great(er) value) and a time charge for Stage 5 Manufacturing and Construction.

Summary of building up a full services fee proposal

This could seem a long and arduous process and you could find yourself flagging if you do not have comprehensive records from past projects for reference. Nevertheless, the aim is to support you in proposing and communicating a fee that represents clear *value* to the client and *fully recognises* the design talent, professional skills and practice experience that you bring to a project in a competitive environment for professional services.

The Project Resources Programme, for example, will tend to follow a pattern, especially for those who work in one sector, such as on small to medium-sized domestic projects. Contractors (and competitors) follow the same process – and in a structured way. *Your contract is your business model* – it is almost impossible to claw back fees later, so treat it like a separate project and give it the time and thought it deserves. In reality, there may be a number of staff planned to work on a project and the simple Programme shown in Figure 4.1 will need to be expanded to reflect the different charge out rates.

Having read this, you may consider a simpler, well-tested method is sufficient for your purposes. This could be to allocate an hourly/daily rate derived from current practice and/or a standard hourly rate (possibly derived by dividing annual revenue by chargeable hours). However, if you want to maximise value – at one end of the scale – or avoid the risk of losses – at the other – it is suggested you link your fee to the factors discussed. Once you know your break-even point and feel familiar with estimating risk, value and profit, this process will become a routine way of setting your standard rates for estimating project resource costs and hence your fees.

Partial services

A fee proposal for partial services can fall into one of several categories:

- Services for specific RIBA Plan of Work stages – for example, Stages 1 to 3 Preparation and Briefing, Concept Design and Spatial Coordination (including planning applications) or Stage 4 Technical Design (including Building Regulations applications) and/or Stage 5 Manufacturing and Construction.
- Specific tasks – for example, feasibility studies (at Stages 0 and 1).
- Specific roles – such as acting as client adviser (potentially working across all stages but in a clearly defined role).
- Specialist services – for example, advising on historic buildings, making grant applications or negotiating complex statutory approvals.

You can approach a fee proposal for partial services using the same process as when building up a full services fee proposal: estimating resource, time and outputs, taking account of the value, risks and a margin for profit. Broad benchmark hourly/daily rates will help you carry out a reality check, but make sure you don't use published percentage fees that are based on a full service.

Your break-even point will be known from the build-up; likewise where you provide added value. A partial service with clearly defined boundaries and outputs (and hence, fewer known risks), such as carrying out a feasibility study, can be treated as a small, self-contained project and be presented as a lump sum fixed fee. However, it is important to build in some risk allowance to cover subsequent actions and to ensure you exclude significant additional work.

Carry out any additional work on a time charge basis upon client instruction, unless you have included in your proposal an allowance for subsequent work which cannot be defined in either time or resource. A halfway house would be to make a lump sum fixed fee proposal for a specific piece of work and then offer further work on a time charge or a further lump sum basis. This provides transparency and the opportunity for further dialogue.

Developer-contractor clients who require services over specific RIBA Plan of Work stages (typically Stages 1 to 4) often ask architects for a lump sum fixed fee in the same way as they would for a subcontractor. In such cases, you will be expected to take account of any project risks without requests for additional

Fee calculation and negotiation: how to put together an effective fee proposal

fees. The more work you do for a particular client, the more the mutual benefits are recognised and the risks reduced.

Specialist services, where you have a particular expertise that exceeds the normal competencies of an architect, are of significant value by definition, and this should be reflected in your charge out rate. If the proposed services do not have any finite time boundaries, a time charge is the most appropriate option. Prospective clients effectively take all the risk and may therefore want to limit the scope. A sensible approach is to suggest a preliminary fee ceiling followed by regular review points.

Entering new sectors

Your practice is likely to initially operate in an area which you understand and where you can navigate comfortably through the local regulatory systems. You may also specialise in a specific sector, such as end-user domestic client projects or small-scale residential developer projects. Through experience, you will come to know where you contribute most value to a project and the appropriate fee. Widening your horizons and entering new sectors presents fresh challenges and time should be set aside to carry out some research.

The limited use of benchmark data in deciding what fee to charge has been covered in Chapter 3; however, the same principles apply. Build up a fee proposal that is based on resourcing, time and outputs. The risks appear higher initially and the value you bring less apparent. It is therefore essential that you understand the prospective client's professional services requirements, as they may be different from your usual practice.

The same principle of aiming to establish a mutually beneficial relationship applies. Dialogue with the client will help to ensure you have fully understood their expectations regarding the services they require in order to achieve their project objectives. To reduce the unknowns, it is important to carry out a comprehensive study of the new area or sector before making a fee proposal. Use the benchmark data as a crude reality check. You may then decide that it is not an area that you want to enter and that the returns relative to the risks are too low.

Alternatively, you can reduce the risks by making use of your professional networks and through informally working with a mentor. Risks could be shared by teaming up with another architect or small practice to prepare a joint proposal, although it is worth noting that this can bring its own challenges and complexities, as the returns as well as the risk must be shared proportionately. Whatever you decide, it is important to be confident that working in a new area or sector will bring satisfactory returns as well as new opportunities to your practice.

Negotiation

In recent years, much research has been carried out into the practice of negotiation. The Harvard Negotiation Project (HNP)[2] classifies negotiators as one of two types: positional or principled. As you gain experience, you will come to identify these two types of negotiator.

- **Positional negotiators** see negotiation as a contest to be won. Typically, they will haggle – sometimes ignoring the merits of your proposal – leveraging the strength of their position as a customer or client. Typically, a developer or contractor with experience in multiple negotiations will maximise their position and exploit the imbalance in bargaining power in negotiation.
- **Principled negotiators** make decisions that are based on merit and mutual gain from the information available and an understanding of the complexities and value of your professional services.

It is fair to expect a client to want to negotiate a fee with you for a number of reasons. They may be positional negotiators by nature, who like to haggle and bargain. If this is the case, once the deal is completed, they tend to stick to the terms of the deal that is struck.

You may be in competition with other architects, designers or contractors. This ought to be declared at the outset, if only as a way of managing expectations. Whether in competition or not, particularly as regards domestic projects, clients will want to be satisfied that they are getting the best value, based on a set of factors or principles, which includes – but is not exclusive to – cost. Prominent among these factors is the relationship-building discussed earlier.

As an architect you will know that your value to a project consists of more than achieving the lowest cost proposal. A key art of successful negotiation is to communicate to the client the added value you bring to a project.

Although negotiations are a common part of life, they are not easy to do well. In a competitive environment, you are expected to negotiate. Hence, it is important your fee proposal is structured in such a way that it sets out a logical, principled approach to the project.

All architects are required to follow the standards set out by the RIBA and the ARB and to act honestly and with integrity. Whether dealing with a positional or principled client, successful negotiation normally has three stages: first, your offer; second, a qualified rejection is made by the client; third and finally, a modified offer is made to the mutual benefit of both client and architect. There may remain small details to be resolved later.

1. Proposal

This is your comprehensive proposal which is based on the method outlined above – or a response to a request for a bid to be made in an agreed format. Bearing in mind the importance of relationship building, this is an opportunity to meet the client and go through the services, the programme, the outputs and the fee, expenses and exclusions. It is also a chance to discuss the design team and consultant appointments.

2. Prospective client response

The client may accept your proposal and proceed to confirming your appointment. Alternatively, they may respond with queries or a straight request to reduce the fee. It can be useful to meet the client and review the fee proposal.

3. Response and revised proposal

Experienced negotiators aim to empathise with the other party and seek to understand their point of view. You should, in like manner, consider how your prospective client is likely to react to your fee proposal. For example, you may have proposed a lump sum fee that is based on your understanding of the brief and estimate of the detailed resourcing required over the likely project programme. Your prospective client may simply convert this into a percentage of *their* construction budget (which could be unrealistic and/or different from the one given to you) and find the result higher than expected. Clients often take advice – possibly from clients you may have recommended they contact – and make comparisons. This is one reason for carrying out the iterative reality check exercise described earlier. At a more nuanced level, your perceived value may neither be fully understood nor appreciated.

There are a number of ways of responding, but do remember that the aim is to arrive at a mutually beneficial agreement. Major revisions to a fee proposal after renegotiation are unlikely to result in a successful relationship, even if you are appointed. Once negotiated, it is difficult to claw back fees as the project progresses. An option is to reduce or omit your fee for a part of the project. If the prospective client offers to pay a fee below your break-even point, you need to consider whether it is worth taking a loss on the project. Whatever you decide, you should not agree to take a position that is unsustainable financially or reduces the service you can offer to below an acceptable level. In either case, you are likely to fall below the standards required by the RIBA and ARB codes of conduct and minimum standards of practice.

To arrive at a successful outcome and maintain a good relationship throughout a project, you must listen to and take account of your prospective client's concerns at this critical stage. Some concerns may be simple queries; some may be due to a lack of understanding about the depth and breadth of the services; for example, the time required to deal with planning authorities. Take this opportunity to explain where you add value. It is important to steer clients towards a principled approach that is based on your proposal and to address their concerns. Some adjustment of the fee may also be needed in recognition of their concerns and to reach an agreement.

Other considerations

Negotiation is commonly considered as taking place before a project has started. However, it can occur at any time, particularly during the later stages of a project. It is very common for architects to raise concerns about clients renegotiating fees towards the end of the project, or simply not paying the final or penultimate fee invoice.

From a positional perspective, the client is in a good place in such cases: they have extracted the key value you brought to the project. They may also consider that, by the later stages, you will have made most of your gains from the project, and that you will be prepared to accept the marginal effect that failure to pay the final invoice(s) in full is likely to have on your overall return and profit. As your involvement reduces, your attention may also have already switched to other projects. Anecdotally, some architects factor this potential loss of fee income into their wider fee calculations. However, it is recommended that you follow a principled, structured approach that is based on your resourcing and the service provided. You may decide to factor the risk of default or delay into calculations, which is of equal importance when appointed for partial services. How to deal with late payment is discussed further in Chapter 7.

Lastly, successful negotiation takes considerable planning and should be treated like a feasibility study, with a range of scenarios and outcomes. Professional negotiators spend the majority of their time planning their approach, and look at the negotiations from both points of view, running through different scenarios and asking 'What will success look like?'

Empathising with the client is important: 'What are they thinking?' 'How will they respond?' Negotiators spend time listening and adapting their responses while knowing the consequences – hence the need for systematic planning.

Summary

Time is your key resource. It is essential that you appreciate the value you contribute to a project and that that value is recognised in your fee proposal using the four variables: time, resource, outputs and Project Resources Programme.

Fee calculation and negotiation: how to put together an effective fee proposal   4

Applying simple risk management methods and estimating risk primarily in terms of fixity or clarity of outcomes serves to identify those areas of greatest risk to you in terms of the time required to achieve outcomes that are often, by their nature, ill-defined.

Your fee should also include a premium for any risk transfer to the architect, such as employing subconsultants. Identifying areas of greatest value helps to maximise your fee. Ideally, you should aim to achieve the greatest value for the lowest risk.

Prepare to negotiate by first empathising with your client so that you can communicate the *value* you contribute through a principled approach. Prepare for different scenarios. Remember that an agreement should be to the mutual benefit of the client *and* the architect. (Otherwise – at worst – you will be unable to meet the terms of the agreement and sustain your practice.)

If final negotiations come down to cost (the positional approach), make use of the different scenarios on which you based your proposal. Finally, if what is offered is below your break-even point, be prepared to walk away. You cannot sustain and grow your practice by subsidising your client.

WATCH POINTS

- Remember, you may be agreeing your fee at the point of greatest uncertainty in the life of a project in terms of its scope, total budget and programme – Stage 0 or 1.
- Bear in mind the differences between the methods of charging in terms of risk allocation. Fee proposals may often include more than one method to suit the balance of risks.
- If you agree to a lump sum fixed fee, try to include terms that allow the fee to be renegotiated if the scope and/or programme should change – otherwise, you carry the risk of change without the option of negotiating additional fees.
- Identify the value you add at the different RIBA Plan of Work stages. Communicate that value and consider pricing your services accordingly.
- Partial services: make sure the outputs are clearly defined.
- Employing subconsultants: consider the liability issues and allow for any additional costs, including the time and costs of administrating and managing subconsultant contracts.

- Always prepare a Project Resources Programme. Consider different project scenarios in terms of programme, outputs and resourcing – and then iterate.
- Carry out a reality check – convert your proposed fee into a percentage and back again.
- Be prepared to negotiate – be principled and plan for different scenarios.
- Remember – it's all about *time*.

Endnotes

1   Many practices will not calculate their fees using the break-even point 'net rate' plus risk, value and profit. They may consider this too time-consuming and use instead past experience as a guide. However, all businesses need to know their exact cost base – especially in a competitive environment. The aim is to create a direct link between effort, value and revenue and to model this so as to potentially increase your profits.

2   The Harvard Negotiation Project (HNP) is part of the Program on Negotiation at the Harvard Law School. It is best known for its theory of principled negotiation – see www.pon.harvard.edu.

5

Resourcing and systems for effective time management

This chapter explains how the Project Resources Programme can help you manage a project once an appointment has been secured and a contract agreed with the client. While your professional services contract will set out the services you are to provide, as well as the programme and scope of work, the Project Resources Programme can be used as a framework for the organisation and monitoring of resources required to deliver those services at each of the RIBA Plan of Work stages.

This chapter explains:

- why having a Project Resources Programme is important
- how to utilise your professional services contract to create a framework
- how to allocate staff resources to a project
- effective time management and the importance of communication with staff
- what to consider when establishing a Project Resources Programme
- how small efficiencies can reap big rewards.

Introduction

In order to manage resources effectively, it is vital that you have a plan. As described in previous chapters, this requires that you confirm the professional services contract in detail sufficient to define the scope of the project and your professional service. You will also have agreed a project programme and the fee to be paid at defined invoice points, ideally monthly. These documents can be brought together to form a Project Resources Programme for in-house resource management. You will need to monitor the plan, keep the client informed of developments and have a change control system that records any divergence from either the scope or the brief and its implications for the cost or the project programme.

Project Resources Programme

The Project Resources Programme is an integral part of your fee proposal. It must cover all the main activities and relevant stages of the RIBA Plan of Work. It will flag up key events, for instance, meetings, planning submission or tender action. It will identify the resources needed to deliver the project in terms of person days per month.

Along with the other documents that form the basis of your professional services contract, the Project Resources Programme provides a datum for any future changes that may occur as the project develops in detail. The Programme itself is a useful planning tool, not only for the design team, but also for the client, since it identifies key RIBA Plan of Work stages and any periods required for design sign off or briefing data.

The RIBA Professional Services Contracts allow key dates from the client's project programme to be inserted, as well as the number of meetings and site visits it is proposed that you will attend. This information can be supplemented by a Project Resources Programme, where you can put on record your understanding of the client's requirements. Agreeing the scope at the outset of a commission provides a datum for any later fee negotiations, should changes occur to the brief.

A Project Resources Programme is the basis of your staff resources plan. It should therefore include the following supporting documentation:

1. A list of the key personnel working on the project and their charge out rates.
2. A schedule of the number of person days that you intend to commit to the project each week/month or for each RIBA Plan of Work stage.

3. A schedule of the information to be produced and other deliverables, with the number of person days assigned to each task.

In Chapter 4, the basis of a fee proposal was discussed, together with a way to build up your fee. Many offices only consider items 1 and 2 above when calculating their fee, relying on general experience to work out the person days required.

Sometimes the procurement route to be taken is undecided initially and therefore assumptions have to be made in order for a fee proposal to be calculated. Putting a marker down early, right at the outset, ensures that any changes to the procurement strategy that have resource implications can justifiably be discussed with the client later.

A critically important issue for any client is the project budget. This should be recorded in the professional services contract. Whether or not your fee is calculated as a percentage of the construction cost, the budget gives an indication of the scale of the project. Sometimes, the client's estimate is an optimistic one and gives a false impression. If you feel that the budget is not viable, it is important to raise this issue and advise that a professional assessment of the cost of the project be carried out.

Use of software systems

There are many software systems available to architects for the planning and monitoring of resources and fees on projects. They range from basic accounting packages to far more sophisticated systems that allow the creation of a detailed plan for monitoring project resources on a weekly basis. Whichever package you choose, it is important to continue to have access to past information, should you decide to stop the service or transfer to another system.

Within the scope of this guide, it is not possible to go into the different software packages in detail. It is, however, necessary that you understand the principles behind them so that the data can be interpreted in an intelligent way. The approach described here does not require a sophisticated system; a simple spreadsheet setting out the target resources for the project week by week should suffice.

Keeping the client informed

Keeping the client informed is good practice. As part of the general management of a project, there will be a series of regular meetings with the client set out in the Project Resources Programme. It is sensible to include client instructions as an item on the agenda for these meetings. This allows you to keep the client up to date and to advise on any changes that have implications for staff resources and fees. This can sometimes be a challenge for sole practitioners working on smaller projects with domestic clients. However, you should try to manage your client, to ensure that any incremental changes do not have an unexpected impact on the overall cost or fee. It's all about managing the client's expectations.

> **CAUTIONARY TALE**
>
> An architect was commissioned for RIBA Plan of Work Stages 1 to 3, to design a riverside development within a conservation area. Following pre-application planning discussions, it became apparent that this was a sensitive location and that the local authority required justification for the approach taken. Other specialists were employed, and the client asked that the architect take them on board as subconsultants, on the understanding that the architect would be reimbursed. The project required a topographical survey, an environmental consultant, an arboriculturist, a structural engineer, a heritage expert, a highways engineer and a planning consultant. At every stage, the architect explained to the client why a specialist was needed, reported the costs and obtained authorisation. The planning application was successful, but the total cost of the other firms was well over twice as much as the architect's fee and a considerable amount of time was spent in managing the team. The moral of this tale is threefold: first, it takes a significant amount of time to manage subconsultants; second, the client needs to be kept aware of the likely final fee across all disciplines; and third, any claims for additional fees for subconsultants have to be filtered and justified to the client by the architect on behalf of the subconsultants.

Effective time management

Time management can be difficult for architects because achieving the right quality sometimes demands more time than originally planned. Nevertheless, your practice is a business, therefore it is important to run it in an efficient way. Having produced a Project Resources Programme, it is sensible to communicate this plan to staff to make them aware of how long has been estimated for certain tasks. Any variance between planned and actual resources can then be flagged up at monthly review meetings (see Chapter 6).

Resourcing and systems for effective time management

Establishing a Project Resources Programme

From a fees and staff resources perspective, there are some key issues to note when developing a Project Resources Programme.

Different RIBA Plan of Work stages carry with them different risks, as discussed in Chapter 1. It may be that, as a practice, you have chosen to take a lenient view of any additional time spent in the interest of securing the commission or out of loyalty to a longstanding client. Where it proves impossible to absorb the additional practice resources spent, the Project Resources Programme is a useful tool for demonstrating to the client where things have changed.

RIBA Plan of Work Stages 1 and 2 require you to have a well-defined brief. It is important to develop solutions that meet that brief and to use the client's sign-off system to confirm that a particular stage has been completed. This is because being asked to look at further design options after client sign off can be costly in terms of resources. Stage 3 can involve lengthy negotiations with the local authority planning department, or extensive community engagement. Setting out a strategy at the outset allows a case to be made for additional fees, should it prove necessary.

Different procurement routes have different resources implications at Stages 3 and 4. Two-stage tendering can involve more work, and a management contract may stipulate that you produce multiple work packages. Being novated to a design and build contractor carries many risks and such contractors vary enormously in terms of the quality of information they expect from an architect. Finally, the programme for Stage 5 is difficult to predict – it can prove both frustrating and expensive in resources when the construction period overruns through no fault of the architect. While there are provisions within professional services contracts for additional fees, Stage 5, when the client is already under stress as a result of the delay, is often a difficult time for the architect to make such a request.

GOOD PRACTICE EXAMPLE

A practice, experienced in dealing with refurbishment projects, provided a lump sum fee to an educational institution for RIBA Plan of Work Stages 1–6 using a traditional procurement route. The fee was built up from the tasks identified and time calculations and a Project Resources Programme was prepared showing key meetings and weekly site visits. During Stage 5 Manufacturing and Construction, a number of difficulties were experienced. Due to examinations taking place in close proximity to the working area, the contractor had to stop work to avoid

> noise disturbance. The building contract period became prolonged, as a result of which the architect had to make 50% more site visits than had been allowed for. The practice was, however, able to negotiate an additional fee because they had set out their fee and service proposal in a detailed manner, supported by a Project Resources Programme.

Allocating resources

The ARB code requires that members consider the resourcing implications of a project and how they might meet their obligations to the client. If you are a sole practitioner, deciding who is to work on a project is straightforward, assuming you have an even flow of work. For larger practices, a decision about which member of staff is assigned can be a difficult one and depend on availability, expertise, experience and programme.

When putting a fee proposal together, you will consider what resources are needed. Often, however, there is a delay between a fee proposal being put forward and the project getting started. During this time other projects may come on stream. A Project Resources Programme means you can see what resources are required and when they are needed. If there is a shortfall in terms of the whole office resources, additional staff may be necessary, impacting on your office finances.

Relating resources to profitability

You will be aware of your break-even point, with allowances for profit, non-productive time and risk. Assuming you have planned the project resources accurately, and the project meets its targets, the project should contribute to the overall practice goals. If the project overspends on resources, you will know that the job is making a loss from the margin you have built in. Running an architectural practice is not a precise science. That being the case, profitable projects are needed as support for those jobs that are overspent.

Change control

Change control is an established project management method. It is applied extensively at RIBA Plan of Work Stage 5 to assess the implications of variations and to make sure that the client is kept informed. Change control techniques can also be used to manage the design process over the earlier stages. When an event or significant design change occurs, the cost, quality

Resourcing and systems for effective time management

and programme implications are established. The client is then advised and asked to authorise the change prior to work taking place. This is the time when you should to flag up any implications this change might have for either your fee or the service agreement. In some circumstances, work may have to stop until the client provides the necessary authorisation.

In order to make a case for additional fees, you will need to show that the client was aware of the change and authorised the extra work. Ideally, reimbursement is on a time charge basis, but sometimes a client will want to agree a lump sum figure instead. Whichever option is chosen, the fee charged should equate to the person days required to carry out the work.

> **GOOD PRACTICE EXAMPLE**
>
> A practice was appointed by a design and build contractor to deal with RIBA Plan of Work Stage 4 Technical Design, for a new entrance to a theme park for which planning approval had been granted. The practice provided a detailed breakdown of their lump sum fee, based upon the tasks and time required and supported by a Project Resources Programme.
>
> Pressure was exerted by the client to deliver the completed project in time for a bank holiday opening. Following the architect's appointment by the contractor, the client instigated a number of design changes that required the practice to spend longer than anticipated on technical design during Stage 4. However, a rigorous system of change control meant that these changes were investigated, assessed and instructions issued promptly, causing minimal disruption to the programme. Stage 5 went smoothly on site and the practice spent less time than anticipated dealing with site queries due to the quality of information they had produced.
>
> The architect kept track of the additional design development time spent on the client variations at Stage 4, but did not feel it necessary to claim for addition fees seeing as, overall, the project had met its office resource targets.

Whole office resource issues

The impact of fees on resources and how projects are managed has a big effect on profitability. Reviewing the overall office picture is important. Projects that have overspent in terms of resources can then be seen in the context of other jobs that were profitable. Whether you decide to make a case for additional fees will depend not only on the validity of the case to be made, but also your relationship with the client concerned, your spread of work and your profit margin. Sometimes projects are accepted with low margins because they are in a sector you wish to enter for the first time, or they will provide a junior member of staff with valuable experience. In such circumstances, it is important to be realistic about resource targets.

Finally, consider where you are adding value to a project. For example, this could be where, despite challenging circumstances, your skill and experience will enable you to obtain planning permission. In such instances, you may choose to adjust your level of fee accordingly. You may also choose to reflect the variation in risk associated with the different RIBA Plan of Work stages in your invoicing; for example, tapering the amount to be charged in the final instalments at the point when the likelihood of non-payment is highest.

The impact of improved performance

Success in business can often be attributed to small improvements in efficiency. These are known as marginal gains. For example, take a small practice with a revenue of £400,000, of which £40,000, or 10%, is profit. If the firm were able to improve its overall efficiency by 5%, this would yield an additional £20,000. Expressed as a percentage of profit, this represents a 50% increase in profit, from £40,000 to £60,000.

In order to manage your business efficiently, it is essential to have a reliable management system. Good monitoring and control may yield marginal gains, which can have a significant positive effect on the bottom line. Similarly, not monitoring may lead to estimated margins disappearing and you working below your break-even point, resulting in a loss.

Summary

The Project Resources Programme is important. It is a key part of your professional services contract and a tool for planning and organising resources. Keeping the client informed and managing expectations is critical. Our projects are all prototypes, and inevitably there will be variations and developments which can sometimes have resource and fee implications for your practice. Finally, your staff are your key asset. It is helpful to involve them in the Project Resources Programme, so they are aware of how each project is to be run.

WATCH POINTS

- Using a Project Resources Programme allows you to monitor resources against a datum.
- Communicate the project plan to staff.
- Keep the client informed – and have a variations tracker.
- Have a system whereby the client signs off each RIBA Plan of Work stage.
- Don't obsess about one project; consider whole office profitability instead.
- Small improvements in efficiency make a big difference to profitability.

6

Monitoring projects, change control and managing fees

This chapter explains how to monitor a project once it is up and running. This can be a challenge. Clients change their minds. Unforeseen problems occur. Because you've spent too long on a project, it becomes impossible to meet the initial resource targets. In order to make a case for additional fees when this happens, you need to be able to demonstrate that you have been involved in extra work, when measured against an agreed benchmark.

This chapter explains:

- why monitoring is important
- how office finances affect resourcing
- the importance of the monthly profitability indicator and work in progress
- how a cash flow forecast works and the importance of working capital
- the key issues to cover in a monthly project review
- how change control can help with additional fee negotiations.

Effective monitoring of projects

Once a job is confirmed it is necessary for you to use the Project Resources Programme as a monitoring tool. This means that the Programme has

Good Practice Guide: Fees

to be simple, accessible and able to be revised. What might have been an excellent plan at the outset can become out of date due to client variations, project creep or delay. By using change control procedures, it ought to be possible to keep the client informed and manage resources effectively. Often it is the client variations that cause an overspend on a project's staff resource allocation and lose money for the practice.

Why cash is important

Cash is king when running a business. Working capital is critical to viability. Some firms fail due to a lack of cash rather than a lack of work. Architects are normally paid in arrears, once the work has been completed. Fee invoices are often in instalments, but it can still take two or three months until payment is received from the client.

The money you need to pay staff and other overhead costs in the meantime is called working capital. Assuming it takes an average of three months to be paid from the time the work was carried out, a firm with revenue or turnover of £500,000 would require working capital of £125,000 to cover this time lag. An efficient office might manage to reduce this period down to two months, but, even so, some client organisations work on a 90-day payment period from receipt of invoice. This could lengthen the time lag to as long as five months, requiring working capital of approximately £200,000. Working capital may be provided as cash from the partners/directors of the firm or as a loan. Whichever system is used, the working capital has a value, therefore it is sensible to keep it to a practical minimum. If you are a new practice without assets, you may have difficulty securing a loan from a bank.

In the following example, problems of cash flow lag cause difficulties for a practice that has secured a large commission.

> **CAUTIONARY TALE**
>
> A small practice expanded following a successful bid for three large commissions from a local authority client as part of a masterplan. Fee instalments were tied into the RIBA Plan of Work stages, meaning that fees were invoiced at the end of each stage. Their payment term of 30 days meant that monies were received two or three months after the actual design work had been completed in the office. This resulted in a cash flow problem and the practice had to negotiate a substantial loan to cover their working capital requirements, for which the bank required security. Had the practice not had the assets necessary to secure the loan, this could have resulted in bankruptcy.

Monitoring projects, change control and managing fees 6

Whole office financial issues

The most important asset of any architect's office is its talent. Whichever way you work out the fee, the expenditure of resources is dependent upon the amount of staff time spent. Chapter 3 explained that whole office costs comprise staff costs, office overheads (including support staff) and profit.

In order to monitor the financial performance of the practice it is necessary to review the following three things:

- a cash flow forecast, which projects forwards in order to get a financial picture of the coming months
- a monthly profitability indicator, which provides a financial snapshot of the business
- the work in progress on projects, which allows the profit to be established.

It is not possible to go into each in much detail, but the general principles need to be understood.

Cash flow forecast

For an office of any size, it is important to know how the practice's bank balance stands in relation to the work expected to come in over the coming months. There are software packages available that do this forecasting for you, but the basic principles are fairly simple (Table 6.1).

An opening bank balance is inserted in the top line of the first month, from which is subtracted the outgoings predicted for that month. To this figure is added the total income expected from fees, resulting in a closing balance. The closing balance is then transferred to the top line of the following month and the whole process starts over again. It is likely that the cost of staff salaries will be similar each month, assuming staff numbers stay the same. However, your other outgoings can vary each month, particularly if some bills are paid quarterly or yearly. Income will be project specific. You therefore need a table showing invoice points for each project (Table 6.2).

Any delays in receiving fees due to programme changes, late payers or bad debts must be incorporated every month to take account of what is actually happening. The same is true of outgoings, particularly if staff numbers change. A cash flow chart can be a proactive tool and a prompt to take action if fees are outstanding.

This exercise will ensure you know how the practice's bank balance is likely to look in the coming months and enable you to take action if necessary.

Good Practice Guide: Fees

Table 6.1: Cash flow forecast for a small practice

Month	January	February	March	April
Opening balance	40,000	45,300	38,000	41,200
Add income from all projects in the month	45,000	40,000	38,000	35,000
Less outgoings in the month				
Partners'/directors' salaries	12,000	12,000	12,000	12,000
Other staff salaries, including National Insurance	18,000	18,000	18,000	18,000
Subconsultants	1,000	2,000	1,500	1,000
Stationery and other consumables	1,000	500	1,000	1,000
Travelling expenses	500	1,000	500	500
Rent and rates	4,000	0	0	4,000
Electricity	0	0	1,500	0
Telephones and IT	0	2,000	0	0
Repairs and renewals	0	1,500	0	0
Bank charges	400	0	0	0
Cleaning	300	300	300	300
Professional subscriptions	2,500	0	0	0
Professional indemnity insurance	0	10,000	0	0
Total outgoings	39,700	47,300	34,800	36,800
Closing balance	45,300	38,000	41,200	39,400

It should also allow you to consider the implications for cash flow of any new commissions or other initiatives.

Profitability indicator

In addition to looking forward, a monthly snapshot of the profitability of your business is essential. It is strongly advised that firms of architects employ accountants to do their end of financial year accounts. The same framework can be used to capture the profitability for each month. This can be done easily using a software accounting package. But even without software, it is relatively straightforward to create a monthly profitability indicator (Table 6.3).

Monitoring projects, change control and managing fees 6

Table 6.2: Cash flow forecast for a small practice – with the income from individual projects shown

Month	January	February	March	April
Opening balance	40,000	45,300	38,000	41,200
Income from projects in the month				
Project A	5,000	5,000	5,000	10,000
Project B	0	0	20,000	0
Project C	20,000	20,000	5,000	0
Project D	10,000	15,000	5,000	20,000
Project E	10,000	0	3,000	5,000
Total income from all projects in the month	45,000	40,000	38,000	35,000
Less outgoings in the month				
Partners'/directors' salaries	12,000	12,000	12,000	12,000
Other staff salaries, including National Insurance	18,000	18,000	18,000	18,000
Subconsultants	1,000	2,000	1,500	1,000
Stationery and other consumables	1,000	500	1,000	1,000
Travelling expenses	500	1,000	500	500
Rent and rates	4,000	0	0	4,000
Electricity	0	0	1,500	0
Telephones and IT	0	2,000	0	0
Repairs and renewals	0	1,500	0	0
Bank charges	400	0	0	0
Cleaning	300	300	300	300
Professional subscriptions	2,500	0	0	0
Professional indemnity insurance	0	10,000	0	0
Total outgoings	39,700	47,300	34,800	36,800
Closing balance	45,300	38,000	41,200	39,400

Table 6.3: Profitability indicator – five months

	1	2	3	4	5	6
Month	Bank balance	Work in progress	Debtors	Creditors	Total	Profit
		Add	Less	Add		
	(the actual amount in the bank)	(work done but not billed yet)	(people you owe money to)	(work invoiced but not yet received)	(an arbitrary figure)	(the 'increase' since last month)
January	33,000	25,000	−10,000	35,000	83,000	
February	36,000	15,000	−5,000	45,000	91,000	+8,000
March	45,000	20,000	−10,000	40,000	95,000	+4,000
April	20,000	35,000	−5,000	40,000	90,000	−5,000
May	10,000	45,000	−10,000	55,000	100,000	+10,000
Total profit (over five months)						+(17,000)

Column 1 of the profitability indicator is the actual amount of money in the bank account at a certain point in the month. Column 2 is the work in progress across all the projects in the office. This figure is the amount of fees earned for which invoices have not yet been submitted. For example, if a project is ready to be submitted to the local planning authority, but the client has yet to approve the drawings, the work in progress will be all the work associated with RIBA Plan of Work Stage 3 undertaken since the last fee invoice.

Column 3 is referred to as debtors. These are people to whom you owe money for goods or services. It is important to consider these liabilities, as some outgoings – such as quarterly rent or yearly professional indemnity insurance premiums – can be relatively large sums.

Column 4 is creditors. These are the people who owe you money, normally clients who have yet to pay a fee account that has been rendered. The assumption is that these are reliable clients and so, although the money has not actually been received it should be included as income at this stage. Adding these four columns together gives a total (column 5) which, when compared with the previous month's total, shows whether you have made a profit or a loss (column 6). A cumulative running total shows profit since the start of the financial year, in which any monthly inaccuracy in the work in progress estimate tends to get evened out.

The monthly profitability indicator is a reminder that just because there is money in the bank it does not mean that the firm is making a profit. Table 6.4 shows the problems encountered by a profitable practice whose costs

Monitoring projects, change control and managing fees 6

Table 6.4: Profitability indicator – eight months

	1	2	3	4	5	6
Month	Bank balance	Work in progress	Debtors	Creditors	Total	Profit
		Add	Less	Add		
	(the actual amount in the bank)	(work done but not billed yet)	(people you owe money to)	(work invoiced but not yet received)	(an arbitrary figure)	(the 'increase' since last month)
January	33,000	25,000	−10,000	35,000	83,000	
February	36,000	15,000	−5,000	45,000	91,000	+8,000
March	45,000	20,000	−10,000	40,000	95,000	+4,000
April	20,000	35,000	−5,000	40,000	90,000	−5,000
May	10,000	45,000	−10,000	55,000	100,000	+10,000
June	−5,000	50,000	−5,000	75,000	115,000	+5,000
July	−15,000	55,000	−5,000	85,000	120,000	+5,000
August	−20,000	60,000	−5,000	90,000	125,000	+5,000
Total profit (over eight months)						+(32,000)

increased during the months of June, July and August because they took on staff as a result of winning some large commissions (as in the cautionary tale above).

The table shows the bank balance going into the red. Unless the practice has cash reserves, or an agreed overdraft facility, this could result in the business becoming insolvent.

Monthly project review

In addition to looking at whole office costs, profitability and cash flow, it is useful to undertake individual project resource reviews every month. Chapter 4 detailed a system for planning resources over the duration of a project, with person days apportioned to each of the RIBA Plan of Work stages. A project review consists of checking the number of person days planned against the actual resources expended.

If a discrepancy is detected at the monthly review, there are several courses of action that can be taken:

Good Practice Guide: Fees

- Has the scope widened? If the answer is 'yes', then have instructions been received from the client and confirmed, and can a case be made for an additional fee?
- If the scope has widened, but no client instructions to that effect have been received, then why is this? How has this happened, and is it something that the client should be made aware of? Advising the client does not, of itself, mean you have a case for additional fees, but it is certainly good practice. It is also sensible to put it on record that the office is spending longer than anticipated, as this may be useful in negotiations later.
- If the scope has not changed, explore why more time is being spent than originally planned. It could be that an inexperienced member of staff is taking longer to complete tasks or that the office underestimated the complexity of the project, or that another consultant or a contractor is causing delay. In these circumstances, there may be limited options for recovering the situation. Nevertheless, it is best to know what is happening.

A monthly review affords a snapshot of every live project in the office. It is hoped that problem jobs will be balanced by more profitable ones.

Communicating with the client

It is good practice to keep the client informed about the development of the project at every RIBA Plan of Work stage. Matters relating to additional fees can sometimes be sensitive issues. Ensuring that you have in place a regular and methodical system for reporting means that matters relating to change control, variations and additional resources can be brought to the client's attention in a professional manner. It is helpful to have a tracker that records key client instructions and variations in the project. The RIBA and ARB Codes require architects to agree increased fees in advance. You may feel it to be inappropriate to contact the client about additional fees for relatively minor changes. Nevertheless, the tracker allows you to discuss matters at an appropriate time with all the facts to hand.

A feasibility study is normally the best way to test out the viability of a proposition and a time charge fee is the best method of charging for one. In the following cautionary tale, the client insisted upon a lump sum fee. However, it is risky to provide a fixed fee proposal when the brief is poorly defined.

Monitoring projects, change control and managing fees

> **CAUTIONARY TALE**
>
> A practice was approached to help an organisation with a funding bid for a rowing club. The client asked for: 'A lump sum fee for just a few sketches and an idea of cost'. The practice provided a fee, but took care to state precisely what their services included, what drawings would be produced and the basis for any cost estimates. It subsequently transpired that there were many complications and restrictions on the site. In order to justify the viability of the scheme, additional consultants were needed, as well as extensive negotiations with user groups and the local authority. The final fee amounted to over three times the initial amount stated. Wisely, the architect updated the client on their increasing fee commitment on a regular basis, waiting for approval before continuing onto the next stage.

Using change control

As shown in Chapter 5, a system of change control can be used to ensure that the client is made aware of all key changes and a record kept of any instructions. Once this system is up and running, it allows variations to be considered in a methodical way. Ideally, you will also flag up the cost to the client, along with any programme implications. In extreme cases, design or construction work may have to stop until client instructions are received. It may not always be appropriate to claim additional fees, but by adopting a change control procedure you can keep the client informed and avoid awkward surprises at the project's end.

Communicating with staff

The extent to which charge out rates and target person day allowances are shared with staff depends upon the management style of the office. It is unfair to criticise staff for taking too long if they are unaware of what assumptions were made when the fee was put together. It is important that staff are appraised of the deadlines and know what resources have been allowed for. Sharing the Project Resources Programme with the team is an efficient way of relaying this information.

Good Practice Guide: Fees

Summary

Maintaining control of projects and the expenditure of resources is an essential part of running a successful business. Monitoring projects against a pre-agreed plan provides early warnings and opportunities to discuss matters with the client. There has to be some leeway when using this information, since architecture is an art, not a science, and there will be times when the project demands extra resources. Nevertheless, it is better to know where you stand rather than get a shock at the end of a project. If an overspend on resources is due to client changes, making a case for additional fees is easier when based upon sound evidence. In addition, a monthly review of the office profitability indicator, as well as cash flow predictions, is an important reality check that should give you confidence that your business is viable and under control.

WATCH POINTS

- Do not progress a project until an agreed plan is in place.
- Keep the Project Resources Programme updated.
- Monitor each project on a monthly basis, identifying any discrepancy in resources compared with the plan.
- Keep your client informed of any changes and advise if additional resources are required.
- Use your cash flow forecast to check the progress of outstanding fees.
- Review your profitability indicator monthly, looking for trends rather than individual monthly performance.
- Share the Project Resources Programme and resource plan with staff.

7

Invoicing and cash flow

Throughout, this guide has emphasised that time is your key resource and shown how your performance or effort across the RIBA Plan of Work stages is reflected in your planning and fee proposals. Earlier chapters have described how you can build up a fee proposal for the mutual benefit of client and architect. The agreed fee ought to represent the value you contribute to a project, your performance over the course of the project programme and the agreed outputs. When and how you charge for the agreed performance, tasks and outputs is discussed in this chapter in relation to the following:

- working capital
- invoicing
- invoice points and the RIBA Plan of Work
- partial services
- working at risk
- change management
- dealing with late payment
- dispute resolution.

Working capital and settlement periods: payment terms

Most small start-up businesses, including micro and small architectural practices, are undercapitalised. This means they lack sufficient financial resources to adequately invest in buildings and equipment. More importantly, they also lack the cash to finance outgoings over the period between having met resourcing performance in terms of outputs and receiving payment; i.e. they lack working capital. Without working capital, the practice cannot survive except by relying on borrowings – typically a bank overdraft. Working capital is also needed to finance short-term future growth in a business. Interestingly, many small businesses emerging from recession fail when their order books grow, having survived up until then through cost-cutting and possibly extended credit. Unable to obtain investment or borrow more at the bank, they fail because they run out of cash and cannot bridge the short-term gap between increased outgoings and payment, even though their medium-term prospects may have never looked brighter.

In architectural practice, as in a majority of businesses, most costs can be forecast accurately and payments are made either monthly or quarterly. However, unlike for many small businesses that rely on regular payments, or even advance payment before delivery (and sometimes manufacturing or production), the fee income of an architectural practice tends to be characterised by relatively large sums paid at irregular intervals. This presents a constant challenge when a practice is undercapitalised: cash held for investment (if any) is continually being consumed by the need for working capital. Without external investment, it takes time to build a sufficient surplus from profits to adequately finance both routine working capital and future growth. When the alternative is to rack up borrowing, it is no wonder that most practices choose to remain small: the short- and medium-term working capital requirements are too high for anything larger. Far better to remain at a size that is comfortable and has lower risks.

> **CAUTIONARY TALE**
>
> A two-director start-up practice was contacted by a hotel company that one of the directors had worked with previously to develop a new 'mini-hotel' design concept for a lump sum fee. The client then asked them to take the design through to Stage 5 on a new site and to work on two further projects at the same time. As a start-up company without any significant cash in the bank or cash flow from other projects,

Invoicing and cash flow 7

> the directors could not secure the bank loan required to employ more staff immediately. They negotiated with the client who fortunately agreed to monthly payments, in advance, for Stages 2 and 3 on the first project and a reduced fee for the other two projects.

The lesson is to highlight the effects of growing too quickly on the working capital required to cover the period between increasing staff costs and receiving fee payments.

The importance of regular invoicing: cash is king

If the main purpose of holding working capital is to bridge the gap between money going out and money coming in, it follows that, if you can reduce the period between resourcing your performance and receiving payment, you can reduce the amount of working capital required to finance the business. The ideal position is one where you agree advanced payment – payment before the services are performed. The next best is regular interim payments that balance, or marginally exceed, the regular project costs; it is, after all, accepted as normal to request interim payments throughout the period of a building contract.

Historically, your practice's revenue may have arrived in irregular – but large – chunks. If you smooth the lumps, you reduce the working capital requirement and can plan your short- and medium-term resourcing more precisely.

Advance payment may be a realistic option. With a new client, paying for a specific piece of work in advance is one way they can confirm their commitment to a project and to the practice. As this benefits the practice by reducing risk and the amount of working capital required, be prepared to offer a discount for advanced payment.

Invoice points and the RIBA Plan of Work

Historically, the standard RIBA Professional Services Agreements set out the key points in the RIBA Plan of Work *when* we charge clients and *what* we charge – normally calculated as a percentage of the total fee (usually, itself a percentage of the construction cost). They also provided for payment as a lump sum and/or a time charge basis where appropriate. This was readily understood by all the major stakeholders and became the industry norm. However, these contracts also apparently valued the earlier stages more highly than the later ones. The assumption was that traditional procurement and full services was standard practice, with the architect as lead consultant. They were neither resource-based nor transparent – there was no link between resource and revenue. This harked back to the days when architects were not in competition and a time when services were based upon a reasonable understanding of what a professional should be paid. Times have changed. We now practise in a commercial, risk-based environment, where competition is the norm and architects, even small practitioners, work as members of a delivery team, often providing only partial services.

The new RIBA Professional Services Contracts are similarly designed for traditional procurement and the default position for *what* you charge remains based on the RIBA Plan of Work stages. These contracts also allow a choice for *when* you charge, ranging from regular periods to the end of RIBA Plan of Work stages or an agreed schedule of payments.

As it is expected that our costs are relatively regular, the default position recommended here is to invoice on a monthly basis. *What* you decide to invoice for should be set out in a schedule of payments (or 'drawdown schedule'). Using your Project Resources Programme, it is possible to link the monthly amounts invoiced to the calculated or estimated resourcing required. Alternatively, you may choose to charge a uniform monthly amount over the course of the Project Resources Programme.

The link between the schedule of payments and the Project Resources Programme is obvious. These two key documents can be used in combination with either a standard RIBA Professional Services Contract, a bespoke client contract or your own letter contract.

Partial services, reports and studies

You may also be providing partial services, such as Stages 1 to 4, for a developer-contractor client or a specific piece of work, such as a feasibility study or a report. The 'what' is set out very clearly. You should also make sure that the 'when' is clear too. It makes sense to link invoicing to delivery of a specific piece of a work. Should it be extensive – or delayed for reasons outside your control – you should provide for monthly interim payments to be made.

Sometimes the amount of work carried out on a project in a particular month will be relatively small. In such cases, the time taken to prepare an invoice may seem disproportionate to the amount. You may also be concerned that invoicing for this amount appears unprofessional or may give out the wrong signals about the practice's finances. Your default position should be to invoice regularly – which normally means monthly. If this is what has been agreed, follow this pattern or else agree bimonthly or quarterly payments with your client before changing the payment regime. Clients do not like shocks; regular, timely requests for payment – even small ones – show a professional approach to running your practice.

If you use a letter contract because it suits the way you work, avoid linking payment to outputs whose completion may be beyond your control. For example, avoid terms such as 'payment is due on receipt of planning approval'. Feasibility studies or client reports may be delayed by factors outside your control; for example, reliance on information from the client or client consultants. Lastly, avoid linking payment to client approval. This may seem sensible when part of a project plan, but can cause problems should the project, for reasons beyond your control, not proceed. You will then have completed work which is no longer of value to the client.

CAUTIONARY TALE

A sole practitioner routinely used a letter contract for small domestic projects. The letter was expressed clearly and included specific payment points. It described the different stages (visiting site, briefing, and so on). The trigger for the first interim payment was: 'Upon client approval of initial design proposal: £xxx.' The architect sent the drawings and an invoice. Inevitably, the client took issue with the proposals and refused to settle the account. From the architect's point of view, they had responded to the brief and delivered what was agreed. From the client's point of view, they were disappointed with the results. As the dispute – over a relatively small sum of money – escalated, it became evident that the client's expectations were unrealistic and could not be met. From a contractual point of view, this was not relevant – the letter contract stated, 'On approval by the client...'.

The two messages to take away are:

- Avoid payment terms that have trigger points outside your control.
- Think carefully about the wording of your contracts: what may seem completely sensible may result in delayed payment or even non-payment.

In the real-life example recounted as a cautionary tale, a dispute might still have occurred because of the client's unrealistic expectations. However, the architect would have been in a stronger position if payment had not been tied to client approval. Note also that, as the piece of work in dispute was relatively small, a lump sum payment would have been more appropriate than interim invoicing. The use of more precise wording, such as 'On completion of initial design proposal', would also have been better and minimised the risk of a dispute.

Cash flow projections, your project pipeline and fees

Our practice model is the aggregate of our core business – design projects: without them, there would be no business. You may supplement your core business with consultancy, which can usefully smooth cash flow, but we tend to rely on our income from projects. Unfortunately for us, projects are characterised as having beginnings, middles and ends, therefore cash flow can be far from continuous. It is difficult for a small practice to estimate project cash flow over the year with any certainty. Working at capacity, there is little scope for growth. By piecing together the Project Resources Programmes for current projects, projects at early stages and prospective projects, you will get an indication of your income and cash flow. Review these Programmes regularly on a weekly and monthly basis, and your cash position possibly daily, even though you may think you have an instinctive picture of the practice's financial position. For example, if you predict that you will reach capacity, you should review your resourcing rates. Keeping your situation under constant review also means you are able to advise clients more accurately, and tells you when you can start projects or whether you need to make a decision about increasing (or reducing) resources.

Working 'at risk' and working for nothing: zero fees

Earlier chapters in this book discussed risk management and how different types of risk should be factored into your fee calculations. They introduced the link between risk transfer and risk acceptance and how this attracts a premium. There is a distinction to be drawn between working 'at risk' (of no payment) and accepting the transfer of project risks, such as obtaining statutory consents.

You may decide to work at risk, where you are prepared to work without payment. It might be part of your business model to gain work. Or you may have no choice: your client wants some work carried out for nothing, perhaps as a risk-free exercise for them to learn about the practice and its design approach. This occurs, in effect, when entering architectural competitions. It can be seen as an opportunity that you might not otherwise get, and therefore worth the risk.

A few watch points.

- Your design ideas are of great value. If you decide to adopt this approach, be wary of how much design value you are prepared to give away.
- Further, consider potential copyright problems. The question you should yourself ask is: 'Can this design proposal be taken and be developed and delivered without any further input from the practice?'

- If the incentive is the prospect of a project, you should aim to factor in the value of the early work – theoretically plus a premium – as part of your fee proposal.
- Using the methodology described above, this premium for the at risk work can be included in your allowance for risk and profit.

It is very high-risk to link your fee to agreeing to obtain development approvals, a process dependent on statutory planning procedures that are entirely beyond your control or influence. You are committing to high levels of resourcing without a time limit. With such high stakes, it is advisable to factor in a significant risk premium.

Whatever you decide to do commercially, remember that you must abide by the professional standards of conduct and practice required by the RIBA and the ARB. Of particular relevance are ARB Standard 4 'Competent management of your business'[1] and RIBA Principle 2 'Competence: 1.2 Members must be able to provide the knowledge, the ability and the financial and technical resources appropriate for the work they undertake.'[2]

Stuff happens: when things do not go to plan

Projects are affected by unforeseen events. Whatever the event and the reason for it, when stuff happens it will affect one or more of your four variables: time, resource, output and Project Resources Programme. A key function and value of your Project Resources Programme is that it provides a baseline. Projects may be postponed or cancelled at key milestone decision points, resulting in a full services commission turning into a partial services one. Significant delay to any of the RIBA Plan of Work stages can cause additional time to be expended, which affects outputs. Changes to the scope by the client affect the resource required, even if they do not significantly alter the construction cost. A prolonged construction period at Stage 5 will add directly to your time and the resource allocated for contract administration in traditional procurement and/or other more limited services, such as site inspection under design and build.

Lump sum, percentage of construction cost and time charge

Chapter 4 explained that the differences between these three different types of contract are characterised by the allocation of risk. If you agree a lump sum fee, you effectively take all the risks of incurring additional costs in relation to the delivery of your services. In order to mitigate these risks, qualify your fee proposal by stating that the lump sum fee is subject to adjustments in scope and change to the Project Resources Programme. This qualification may or may not be accepted. (If in doubt, take legal advice.) The RIBA Professional Services

Contracts also provide for fee adjustment, but this needs to be agreed with the client beforehand.

Disagreements about the reasons for change

Clients are unlikely to dispute the *amount* of time or resource you claim to have expended. They are more likely to disagree about where *responsibility* lies for an increase in time spent or delay. It is therefore essential to keep good records, continuously recording performance and monitoring it against your plan. The impacts of changes to the scope of the project on design development and your time and resourcing need to be communicated back to the client. To do this effectively, introduce basic change management, where changes are tracked against both the original agreed summary brief and the Project Resources Programme. Not all changes will affect the fee. Use your judgment to determine if and when to raise the question of additional costs with your client.

A review of the source of complaints about the profession – almost entirely from domestic clients – identified particular risk areas. Among these are the following:

- additional design development work at Stages 2 and 3
- protracted planning negotiations at Stage 3
- value engineering post-tender at Stage 4.

As these are regular catch points, it is worth examining them in detail. A good starting point is to remember that a claim for additional fees is essentially part of the same process of negotiation you carried out when the fees were initially agreed. You need to be prepared to set out your stall by keeping records of resources and time spent, allocating these to the relevant RIBA Plan of Work stage and correlating them with the relevant outputs. Again, do not forget to empathise with the client. An appreciation of their point of view can help you frame any claim in terms of the added value to the client, rather than making the mistake of presenting it purely as an additional cost to you and your practice. Remember the principle: an agreement must be seen as a transaction for mutual benefit. The additional work you carry out must demonstrate additional value to your client.

Design development

The blurring of the lines between client changes to the brief, constructive dialogue and additional design development beyond what would normally be expected is potentially contentious. This is partly due to clients not fully understanding either the scope or the intense iterative processes that comprise design development. As recently highlighted in the courts,[3] it is vital that clients are kept informed of continued design development, especially if it takes the design in a different direction to the one initially envisaged. If their value is to be acknowledged, the added value of these essentially internal decisions has to be communicated. Good record keeping is only a start – you need to obtain agreement to achieve consensus. If you keep your client informed and alert them to when you are spending more resource on design development that *might* result in additional fees but *will* add value, the client then has an opportunity to instruct you to continue, review progress or stop work. Regular design review meetings at Stage 2 allow both client and architect to review design development. It is better to deal with additional work through regular routine meetings than flag it up as a one-off problem. Explaining design development to your clients shows them the relatively high value you can contribute to both the project and its lifetime use by a comparatively small marginal increase in the time spent (and hence fees charged) at Stage 2.

> **CAUTIONARY TALE**
>
> At the end of Stage 2, a small practice issued an invoice to a client for additional design development work on a small house extension. The client refused to pay and complained that they had not been told about any additional work and that they expected the design would develop and change – and this is what they had been led to expect when they met to discuss the project initially. Furthermore, they were disappointed about the lack of communication so far and the time it had taken to send the drawings. The director working with the client forwarded it to another director for review and advised the client to that effect. The reviewing director went through the records and, although they could not find a paper trail of discussions with the client or a record of their approval of changes to the brief, it was clear that the design drawings had been changed and sent to the client. They therefore considered that the additional fees were justified. The partner responsible replied formally to the client, dismissing their complaint and finishing his letter with: '... and that is the end of the matter'. It was not. The client complained to the ARB and the architect received a reprimand for failing to communicate regularly with the client and advising them of additional work affecting the cost of their services.

First, it is important to note, with regard to this last cautionary tale, that the practice in question had a complaints procedure in place – even though there were only two directors. Even if you are a sole practitioner, you still need such a procedure in place – ideally, with the aid of another architect you know and with whom a formal reciprocal arrangement can be agreed. Second, it is not unusual with domestic clients for there not to be comprehensive records of design development changes, nor any formal communication of those changes. However, this does leave you vulnerable. Create a change control log or register, update it and regularly update the client. As in collaborative building contracts, such as NEC forms, an early warning procedure flagging the effect of change on cost and time is essential in your professional services contract. This is far better than a claim for additional fees. Lastly, the high tone taken and lack of dialogue between architect and client only led to further problems. Instead of closing it down as intended, it escalated the problem. It is far better to discuss the problem with your client when this happens.

Planning negotiations

Seen from the client's point of view, a key part of your value to a project is the experience and professional judgment you bring to bear in agreeing a design proposal that has a realistic prospect of obtaining consent, then navigating your way through the legislative framework and successfully negotiating the necessary statutory consents. Architects know the risks associated with the development control and heritage application processes.

Pre-application advice is intended to reduce those risks, but the consent decision remains outside the control of the architect and local authority professionals: it is a democratic process and the final decision is taken by the elected committee. Sometimes we architects receive conflicting or inconsistent advice at each stage. Sometimes we advise our clients to take independent action to reduce the risk. You may also need to factor in extensive consultation at the outset. You may also be advised by the local authority to withdraw the application.

The worst case is to receive a refusal that requires extensive redesign, resulting in abortive and additional work and/or an appeal. You are not responsible for the planning decision; the risk remains with your client. However, another way of looking at this is that you have both experienced a disbenefit; your client does not have planning consent and, until consent is granted, you do not have a project.

At worst, you may not have invoiced your client for this activity and there could be a dispute. The equitable way of negotiating your way out of this could be to accept that you carry out a defined piece of work either at cost or at no charge to the client. The danger in this approach is that it can be seen as accepting some responsibility for the failure of the planning application. The benefit is the lasting goodwill and mutuality it can foster – 'we are in this together – let's sort it out'. Some practices even make planning appeal applications at no cost – it is part of their business model. We cannot recommend a correct approach. It will depend on the context and the client's attitude to planning risk (for example, you may have both agreed that there is a significant risk of refusal). What we are suggesting is that working towards a mutually beneficial solution is always worthwhile for sustaining a continued, successful client–architect relationship.

Value engineering

Value engineering (or cost reduction) may occur at any stage, but usually happens if the construction contract tenders obtained at Stage 4 significantly exceed the estimated construction cost previously agreed with the client. The initial client response is often to blame the design team or, for a small project without a cost consultant, the architect. The architect has a professional duty to provide appropriate professional advice. A significant number of complaints about the profession result from a disparity between the architect's advice on the construction cost (at Stages 1 to 4) and the tenders received. The design decision-making affecting the construction costs is seen as being under your control. The prospect of additional fees for redesign work, with the aim of bringing costs back within the total project budget, is difficult for a client to embrace at this stage. The only ways additional fees are clearly justified at this stage are: (1) if the client never made it plain what their budget was, and/or (2) if the client continuously added to or changed the design without adjusting their budget accordingly. In either case, you will need recourse to a clear record of the changes made and your advising that the construction cost will be affected.

You are usually in this position because the construction market is beyond your control. However, the client will expect you to know the market sufficiently well to be able to give accurate advice that can be relied upon. Again, it is impossible to recommend a correct approach to this matter, but the principle of mutual benefit continues to apply. It may be necessary though to demonstrate goodwill in the short term for the sake of longer term benefits to both the project and the client–architect relationship. A significant number of projects never get beyond this stage. Contributing to a successful outcome by being proactive and negotiating with tenderers and subcontractors in order to achieve the most cost-effective solutions may be to the lasting benefit of the project and you may want to take this into account.

Two-stage tendering

Two-stage tendering requires considerably more time in preparing packages and administration than simple, single-stage tendering. It is further complicated by the different approaches to two-stage tendering. It is advised that you try to confirm this requirement as early as possible.

Working at RIBA Stages 5 and 6

Under traditional procurement, the architect is usually the contract administrator for the building contract. However, there may instead be a project manager who carries out this role, or the client may decide they will deal directly with the building contractor. You may still be appointed as a client adviser, to attend meetings, carry out site inspections and give advice to the contract administrator. This work either should or will have been agreed when you prepared your fee proposal. You can estimate the amount of work required, how frequently it occurs and over what period. However, these three factors are in part determined by the performance of the contractor, the number of changes instructed by the client during the construction phase and the quality of the work, all of which are outside your control and therefore potentially high-risk. Moreover, the input of the architect may be seen as having a relatively lower value. For these reasons, it is recommended that you aim to agree at the outset either a time charge for this work or a lump sum fee linked to the building contract period estimated in your Project Resources Programme. You will incur extra direct costs if the building contract period is extended, either due to agreed time extensions or delay caused by the non-performance of the contractor. It is not untypical to experience performance or quality problems towards the end of the construction phase, which may result in a claim by the contractor for additional time and/or money. The client will usually be unhappy, wanting practical completion and occupation as soon as possible. Faced with a dispute, which may rightly or wrongly include a claim for late information or design changes, it is difficult to explain to a client that additional costs have been incurred beyond your control and the result is additional fees, unless this was made clear at the outset and you have been submitting monthly invoices during the construction phase.

Changes to the project that affect your services

Sometimes, for reasons completely outside your control, a project may start well and then take a different turn – one that directly affects your current and future work. For example, you may have agreed to traditional procurement requiring your involvement across all the RIBA Plan of Work stages at the initial briefing meetings and then the client decides to change to design and build or to employ the contractor direct for Stage 5.

GOOD PRACTICE EXAMPLE

A small practice had a framework agreement with a local university. It put in a full services bid for a new laboratory building on a percentage fee with staged payments based upon reaching agreed milestones.

The practice proceeded with the work. It encountered difficulties with the planning authority, but eventually the project was granted planning

> consent. At this point, the university decided to review the project and instructed the practice to stop work.
>
> The practice had spent considerably more time on the project than it had originally planned – or invoiced for – and was losing money on the project. It had hoped to recoup these costs during Stages 4 and 5. It decided to notify the university about the problem and made a claim for additional fees in connection with the planning negotiations up to the agreed milestone, based on its time records and a planning change log. The university agreed to reimburse the practice at a set rate.

The key point to take away from this example is that it is always sensible to discuss recouping costs with the client first, especially when it is a valued client with whom you are hoping to maintain a long-term relationship. The claim was based on accurate records and was presented professionally.

Slow payers: getting paid and dispute avoidance

Following the principle that cash is king, it is important that you chase late settlement of invoices. If keeping to the discipline of monthly invoicing, you should set aside a regular time to review and chase up outstanding accounts. It is suggested you take three simple steps:

Step 1 **Send the client a factual reminder on or before the due date**

The invoice may have been raised four weeks ago for work carried out as much as four weeks before the date of the invoice. It could be a simple oversight.

Step 2 **Send a follow-up email after a further 14 days have elapsed accompanied by a statement of account**

Ask whether there is a problem and how you can assist.

Step 3 **After a further 14 days have elapsed, suggest a meeting to discuss any problems and resolve any issues**

An offer to meet will often highlight any problems or precipitate action. From a client's point of view, there may be advantages to settling your account rather than meeting. Alternatively, it is an opportunity for them to air their views. Although potentially uncomfortable, this will at least give an indication of the likelihood of full payment, or any payment. Avoid protracted arguments conducted by email. You might win the argument, but this may not produce a successful result. It is far better to meet face-to-face. If the client refuses, consider further action.

> **GOOD PRACTICE EXAMPLE**
>
> A small practice completed a feasibility study with a number of options for a niche furniture retailer. The company was headed up by an entrepreneur who had built up the company and was planning to expand on its existing site. The project went quiet and the client did not respond to reminders. One of the practice directors arranged to meet them. The retailer explained that they did not think that any of the designs presented suited their requirements and they saw little value in the exercise. It also emerged that the company had shelved its plans to expand. The architect talked through the options, using this as an opportunity to explain the potential value of the exercise and that the work could always be developed further in the future. The client conceded the value of the work and agreed to settle the account immediately. The architect was successful because they listened to the client's concerns and showed an understanding of their point of view. The architect then tailored their response so as to show the value that they had added, emphasising tactfully that they had followed the instructions and options for the brief, in discussion and as agreed.

Sometimes your client may have hit an unforeseen problem that affects payment. Offering staged payments can build goodwill for the future and may be the best option under the circumstances. It is worth suggesting.

> **GOOD PRACTICE EXAMPLE**
>
> A small practice completed a small office fit-out project for a two-person financial start-up company following a referral from an established client. The company, which appeared well-resourced, hit an immediate cash flow problem due to non-payment of an early client account and asked whether they could delay payment for two to three months.
> The architect agreed. The start-up then grew significantly. Further work followed from the start-up – and from the referral client.

Threatening legal action weakens the client–architect bond. It may also give rise to a counter-claim. You should see the problem as another phase of negotiation. You should take a principled approach, but your client may take a positional stance. A compromise may need to be reached in order to obtain payment. Anecdotal feedback from practitioner CPD sessions has indicated that this is relatively common behaviour among some – but by no means all – clients.

Invoicing and cash flow

At some point you will need to weigh the effort involved in trying to achieve settlement of an account against the effect it might be having on delivering current projects or getting new work.

Dispute resolution

Disputes occur when neither you nor the client can agree on a resolution to what might have started out as a relatively straightforward claim for additional fees or non-payment of fees due. It is always best to try to retain control of the process, in the first instance, through negotiation and/or mediation, rather than passing it onto another person to decide. It is important to make the point that, even with adjudication or a claim in the small claims court, a dispute will significantly slow down payment.

A dispute over payment is almost certain to result in a counter-claim against your performance. Notify your professional indemnity insurer as soon as you think there may be a dispute. They can offer advice based upon extensive experience and, if necessary, will take control of the dispute. Your financial exposure is then limited to the excess. However, you will never be able to charge for the significant time spent making a claim and preparing a case. Again, this issue has a disproportionately negative effect on sole or small practitioners. It is sometimes difficult to remain objective and to compartmentalise a dispute; it can affect your day-to-day performance and morale for the worse. It is far better to avoid a dispute by managing your client's expectations.

Summary

The essential factor ensuring continued success in practice is cash flow. It has been shown that different types of contract have different risks. If you agree to lump sum fees, be clear about the scope and the programme. Careful planning is essential, but projects never go to plan. It is therefore vital that you monitor your resources against your plan – even when the contract is based on a lump sum fee and there is no provision made for change. This at least gives a true picture of whether you are breaking even or losing money.

As projects are prototypes, things change. Always keep your client informed and aim to build a professional relationship with an element of goodwill. Remember that the work you carry out should be for mutual benefit. Whatever the merits of a claim, a dispute will always slow down payment and risk the future relationship. Aim for informed, reasonable dialogue supported by good recordkeeping of your resources: it's all about time.

Good Practice Guide: Fees

> **WATCH POINTS**
>
> - Regular invoicing helps in managing working capital requirements and cash flow.
> - Establish regular invoicing points at the outset.
> - Avoid linking payment points to critical project events that are beyond your control, for example, a funding approval or granting of planning permission.
> - Consider fee risks and how they are allocated; negotiate the option to review a lump sum fee if the project scope, budget or programme changes significantly.
> - Change management: keep accurate records, monitor against the Project Resources Programme and notify your client early if significant variations are likely to affect costs.
> - Be clear about the scope of and deliverables for partial services.
> - Treat payment problems as a negotiation – consider making compromises to secure immediate payment.
> - Formal dispute resolution procedures will slow payment, introduce risk and soak up valuable, non-recoverable resource.
> - Aim for dispute avoidance.

Endnotes

1. ARB, *Architects Code: Standards of Professional Conduct and Practice* (London: ARB, 2017), p 5. Available at: www.arb.org.uk/architect-information/architects-code-standards-of-conduct-and-practice [17 August 2020].
2. RIBA, *Code of Professional Conduct* (London: RIBA, 2019), p 9. Available at: www.architecture.com/knowledge-and-resources/resources-landing-page/code-of-professional-conduct [17 August 2020].
3. *Riva Properties Ltd & Others* v *Foster + Partners Ltd* [2017] EWHC 2574 (TCC).

8

Putting it into practice: a case study

Scenario

The following scenario describes a RIBA Chartered Practice with two directors, a Part 1 student and a part-time administrator-assistant. The practice has been operational for five years, focusing on the design of low/zero-carbon buildings and has a reputation for high-quality individual houses. Projects are generally obtained through a mixture of word-of-mouth recommendation, the practice's website, social media and local profile. The practice's turnover, which had grown for the first three years, has plateaued at approximately £350,000 per annum, and the practice has cash reserves of £30,000.

The potential project

The practice is contacted by a couple who obtained its details through the RIBA Find an Architect service (www.architecture.com/find-an-architect). Although a RIBA Chartered Practice, this is the first time the practice has been approached through this service, so it is likely that they are in competition with other firms.

The couple have bought a small house on a large, sloping plot in a rural location overlooking the sea close to a small village. There are other two-storey detached houses in the area.

Good Practice Guide: Fees

In the initial meeting, the practice stresses its low-energy, zero-carbon sustainability ethos and its track record in delivering innovative projects, both new-build and retrofit. They explain that this approach can increase the construction cost, but that this is offset by reduced operational costs and a minimal carbon footprint.

The architects give an overview of the RIBA Plan of Work 2020 and explain how their professional service works, together with the benefits of the traditional procurement route in achieving quality via a network of reputable local contractors and specialist subcontractors.

The client's brief is to extend the size of the house to accommodate future needs. They have a budget in mind of £500,000, inclusive of fees and VAT, and would like building work to be completed within six months. The couple would like ideas about the potential for improving and modernising the building. They have already met with one architect and are due to meet with another shortly. The couple are currently staying in rented accommodation.

At this stage there is no real brief or scope of services. The architect explains that they may require planning consent for any proposed work, and at this stage they cannot comment on the budget, but that the timescale seems optimistic.

Given the fluid nature of the brief, the architect recommends a feasibility study to explore three options. Following completion of the study, it will be possible to provide a further fee proposal for full services that is based on the budget once the scope of the project is clearer.

The fee proposals

The main problems are that there is no real definition of the project, the budget may be unrealistic and the project timeline seems unachievable. This is a highly fluid and unbounded situation, and therefore high-risk in terms of the unknowns. In order to make sense of a project, you need to establish clear boundaries. The best way to do this is to conduct a feasibility study.

Feasibility study

Ideally, the feasibility study would have been carried out on a time charge basis, but the client insists on a lump sum fee proposal for the study. They identify three options:

1. Extend the house and retain most of the existing features.

Putting it into practice: a case study

8

2. Extend and substantially remodel the house, and upgrade the fabric of the building.
3. Demolish the house and construct a new dwelling to higher standards.

Feasibility studies can vary widely, so it is best to set out exactly what the commission will include, detailing the outputs and exclusions (e.g. protracted planning investigations are excluded). Establishing the boundaries reduces the risk and manages client expectations. A finite product delivered within an agreed timescale is the aim.

The feasibility study fee is calculated on a time basis by identifying the tasks involved. Initially the fee is calculated at cost, based on a break-even point established using the practice's financial data (Table 8.1).

Table 8.1: Office finances

Office finances: three-person micro practice	
Annual revenue	£267,000
Cost of all fee-earning staff	£150,000
Overheads, including admin staff costs	£77,0000
Total outgoings	£227,000
Profit	£40,000

Charge out rate calculation

Fee-earning staff costs: 2 × partners @ £60,000 + 1 × assistant @ £30,000 = total £150,000	
Total outgoings	£227,000
No. of staff	3

	Partner 1	Partner 2	Junior
Proportion of outgoings	2/5	2/5	1/5
Cost to office per year	£90,800	£90,800	£45,400
Break-even point per day (divide year by 227 days)	£400	£400	£200
Break-even point per hour (divide day by 7)	£57	£57	£29
Hourly charge out rate incl. 15% profit	£67	£67	£34
Hourly charge out rate incl. 15% risk	£79	£79	£39
Daily charge out rate incl. profit and risk	£552	£552	£256

Note: As part of the negotiations with the client for the project, the architect agrees a 10% reduction in their fee, reducing the risk element from 15% to 5%, resulting in a new daily charge out rate of approximately £500, which they then use for their Project Resource Programme calculations (the break-even point remains the same at £400 per day).

Good Practice Guide: Fees

The commission allows for three meetings with the client, the first to agree a brief, the second to discuss options and the third to present a preferred option. Any further work is to be by agreement.

The practice has a choice that depends on how much they want the work. They may decide to put in a bid at cost, or possibly below cost, or to apply a margin for profit and risk. However, this early design work is of high value and there is a risk that the client may take the ideas and choose another architect or builder to develop them and implement the scheme.

Knowing that there is competition, the practice could opt to go in at cost. The risk premium is low, but the work is of great value. A problem with going in at or below cost is that this sets a precedent for the rest of the project.

Reality check

The practice carries out a reality check that is based on the hours spent on similar studies. By being specific in the proposal about the deliverables, the unknowns are reduced and the architect remains in control of the resources. The proposal states clearly that the study will comprise only schematic plans and one simple 3D sketch and gives an example from a previous commission in order to manage client expectations. The fee proposal is well-considered and professional.

The client accepts the lump sum feasibility study fee proposal. The practice draws up a letter contract for this commission.

There is no standard RIBA contract for this piece of work. The letter contract must meet the requirements of the ARB Standard 4.4 and RIBA Principle 2. It is classed as a consumer contract.

The feasibility study results in three options:

Option 1   Minimum solution, with a two-storey extension providing an extra bedroom and an enlarged kitchen and utility room at an estimated cost of £250,000.

Option 2   Remodelling of the house with improved fabric and a two-storey extension as option 1 at an estimated cost of £500,000.

Option 3   Demolition of the existing house and construction of a new-build low-energy building designed to Passivhaus standards at an estimated cost of £600,000.

(All figures exclusive of professional fees, disbursements and VAT where applicable.)

The project construction cost estimates for each option are based on a cost per square metre, adjusted for the site location and site conditions, plus

Putting it into practice: a case study

demolition and strip-out costs. Risks relating to ground conditions and the potential discovery of asbestos are excluded and the level of accuracy is clearly stated.

The client likes option 3 (the new-build solution) and they discuss the possible addition of a family room located in a semi-basement, to take advantage of the sloping site and views out to sea.

The added complexity to option 3 requires discussions with the planning authority and the extra professional time involved cannot be accommodated within the initial feasibility study fee.

By referring to the original fee proposal, which shows in detail how the professional time is broken down, the client agrees to additional fees, which the practice then confirms in writing.

This is a way of building a rapport with your client, gauging their appetite for risk and their approach to the realities of a construction project. Also, start a change control register for the project. Even if the project does not proceed, you will have a record as reference for future projects.

At the completion of the feasibility study, the client approves the new-build solution with the family room and accepts the estimated construction cost of £700,000.

There are many things about the brief that remain to be developed, as the client did not really know exactly what they wanted. So there are still risks associated with taking the project forward.

Note: The new estimated total project costs are now significantly higher than the client's original budget of £500,000 including fees and VAT. This is a reminder that it can be unwise to give a lump sum quotation for fees that is based on a budget that does not have any detail. Clients tend to remember the first figure quoted by the architect. If the scope and complexity increase, you will need to explain why your fee will be different. You can also expect your client to adopt an increasingly risk-averse approach, as it is now a very different project from the one they initially had in mind in terms of its scope, budget and programme. The client will need to be convinced of the value that additional project costs, including additional services, will add to the project.

The client requests a lump sum fee for a full service from RIBA Plan of Work Stage 1 to Stage 7 on a traditionally procured basis. They confirm that they want a zero-carbon building and accept that this will incur additional costs compared with a less energy-efficient design.

The architect explains how the RIBA Plan of Work 2020 operates and the general options for procurement. In this case, traditional contracting with some

103

contractor-designed elements would seem appropriate because it gives the client control over the design decisions and selection of specialist elements, as well as the flexibility to change the design, if required.

The practice also outlines the health and safety duties imposed by the Construction (Design and Management) Regulations 2015, specifically the requirement to appoint a principal designer.

Estimating the fee

The fee is calculated using the hourly/daily rate break-even point plus a risk allowance of 15% and a markup for value and profit of 15%.

The fee proposal comprises the following:

1. The scope of services – including the key programme dates.
2. The Project Resources Programme, with RIBA Plan of Work stages and activities, including meetings and outputs.
3. Lump sum fee broken down into four elements: RIBA Stages 1 to 3; RIBA Stage 4; RIBA Stages 5 and 6; and RIBA Stage 7.
4. An invoicing schedule showing monthly payments.
5. Expenses.
6. Exclusions (i.e. other consultants' fees, surveys, local authority planning and Building Regulations fees, etc.).
7. Other (unspecified) services are to be on a time charge basis.
8. A covering letter referring to the use of the RIBA Domestic Professional Services Contract (PSC) and stating that the fee proposal excludes the appointment of other design team consultants (e.g. cost consultant, structural engineer, MEP consultant) and the cost of a topographical survey and ground investigation.

Client response

The client comes back and wonders whether the practice is able to move on fees.

Note: This is the positional approach discussed in Chapter 4 – one not based on the merits or content of the proposal but on position as a potential client.

The practice counter-bids, explaining that the fee proposal has been carefully considered, is realistic and based on previous similar projects. Any reduction would be marginal in relation to the total project budget (a principled approach), the practice stressing their keenness to carry out the commission.

The client then carries out their own reality check on the project with reference to local estate agents to see whether they are likely to recover their costs. They also obtain two other fee quotations. One is 20% lower and on this basis they ask the practice to reconsider its fee.

Client negotiations

In consideration of the break-even point, there is no way the practice can match the competitor's offer; however, the project would be a great addition to its portfolio and the client seems reasonable. After some discussion, the practice agrees to a reduction of 10% (see Figure 8.1, page 112). (The original fee included 15% for risk and 15% for value and profit. In the practice's view, this revised arrangement reduces the risk allowance to 5%.)

By calculating its fee in this way, the practice has an idea of the effect of the negotiation on the allowances for unknowns and profit.

The client queries the need to appoint a cost consultant and an MEP consultant, as they are unconvinced as to the value they bring to the project, and are therefore not prepared to pay for their services. The practice points out that it would be prudent to take specialist cost advice at critical stages. The client suggests the practice appoints a cost consultant at its own expense, and points out the reference to cost reporting in the RIBA PSC as being part of the architect's service. Eventually the client agrees to pay for surveys, a structural consultant and an MEP consultant, while insisting that these should be subconsultants to the architect's practice.

The practice considers that some cost advice is needed at critical stages of the project in accordance with the services set out in the RIBA PSC. Now this is a direct cost to them, it is necessary that the practice factor it in.

Subconsultants are a disproportionate risk to micro-practices, and it may be necessary to speak to the professional indemnity insurer regarding the surveys and the structural engineer's appointment. The risk can be reduced by using a standard subconsultancy contract, such as the RIBA Subconsultant Professional Services Contract. In addition, a collateral warranty serves to establish a direct relationship between the client and the structural engineer/surveyor. Risk transfer attracts a premium and this should be added to the fee.

The RIBA Domestic Professional Services Contract

The client appoints the architect using the RIBA Domestic Professional Services Contract. The Contract Details are based on the following information.

1. The Project Brief

The demolition of the existing dwelling on the site and the design of a four-bedroom house with a semi-basement family room.

2. The Schedule of Services is based on traditional procurement

- Schedule of Services in accordance with the RIBA PSC framework
- single-stage selective tendering
- demolition and site works (services) and new build
- JCT Intermediate Building Contract with contractor's design, with a 12-month rectification period, signed as a simple contract.

3. Project Programme

A Project Programme setting out time limits to the construction programme.

4. Resourcing and deliverables

A schedule of outputs, drawings, specification, schedules.

5. Fee schedule: invoices to be raised monthly

Architectural services

Architect's Basic Fee:

- lump sum for Stages 1 to 3 (£25,000)
- lump sum for Stage 4 (£44,000)
- lump sum for Stages 5 and 6 (£20,000)
- lump sum for Stage 7 (£2,000)

Total architect's Basic Fee: £91,000 (i.e. 13% of £700,000 estimated Construction Cost)

Expenses: £2,000

Other Services

Principal Designer services: £4,000

Consultants and surveyors to be appointed via the architect:

- topographical survey: £1,000
- ground investigation: £3,000
- cost consultant (cost to be borne by the architect)

- structural engineer: £15,000
- services engineer: £15,000

Total for consultants and surveyors: £34,000

Administration fee for consultants and surveyors @ 5%: £1,700

Total for Other Services: £39,700

Total fee: £132,700 excl. VAT

A reality check puts the architect's fee at 13% of the estimated Construction Cost, plus the fee for taking on the Principal Designer role. However, it is based on a bottom-up, detailed approach, so that the practice is confident the service can be delivered for this amount. A considerable amount of effort has gone into putting the fee together, but it does mean that the practice can readily monitor fees and costs during the project against the Project Resources Programme.

The project

RIBA Plan of Work Stages 1 to 3

The design development stages of the scheme go smoothly, with the client being both reasonable and professional in their approach. Some additional time is spent dealing with Project Brief development, and design changes are recorded in the change management register and reviewed regularly.

The practice undertakes pre-application meetings with the planners and the approval process is reasonably smooth-running. The semi-basement family room turns out to be straightforward from a local planning perspective, since it does not affect the overall height of the building.

The practice provides regular project cost updates at the RIBA Plan of Work stages and the change management register is reviewed to detect any impact on the budget.

Unforeseen events

One of the risks identified in the client meetings is the demolition of the existing house. The survey showed asbestos in the building. However, the schedule of services states that the fee is based on single-stage selective tendering. A separate demolition contract might help reduce the risk of delays to the overall programme, but it would also result in more work for the practice. While this is a sensible suggestion, administering a demolition contract requires additional time which is not factored into the original fee proposal. The client is unwilling to agree to extra fees, so this option is not pursued.

There are benefits to reducing project risks. This is a relevant additional service, requiring extra resource and time, for which an additional fee would be due. This could be dealt with as a lump sum calculated on the estimated resource and time needed to deal with the demolition contract. The client could then make an informed choice, weighing the reduced risks against the additional fee costs.

RIBA Plan of Work Stage 4: Technical Design

The design team move on to Stage 4.

The practice makes the Building Regulations application. Prior to tendering, a Stage 4 review shows the pre-tender estimate of the Construction Cost is now £750,000. This is higher than the original budget due to the agreed changes recorded in the change management register. The client reluctantly accepts. A contingency sum of £25,000 is included within this figure.

The project is tendered to five contractors. Two drop out, citing the specialist skills needed to achieve the required performance standards and the scope of the MEP package. Three tenders are submitted, ranging from around £850,000 to £950,000 – well above the client's agreed revised budget. The contractors' programme is in line with the estimated construction period set out in the Project Programme. The client is very concerned, speaks of cancelling the project and insists on an explanation. The Passivhaus features appear to add to the construction cost, together with the family room retaining wall, and the high specification agreed with the client for the kitchen and bathroom fit-out also contribute to the increase.

A meeting is arranged with the contractor who submitted the lowest tender and various value engineering options are considered, as well as a simplification of the building fabric details. After two weeks of redrawing details and negotiation, savings of around £50,000 are agreed, with a revised Construction Cost of £800,000. This is still over the pre-tender cost estimate of £750,000, despite all the contingency having been used up.

The client reviews the situation. After a month they come back, stating their intention to proceed, but proposing to make the kitchen and bathroom ex-contract, getting the fittings installed by their own tradespeople. After a further negotiation with the lowest tenderer, these elements are taken out of the contract and a revised Construction Cost of £700,000 agreed.

Note: On non-domestic commissions, the RIBA Standard PSC provides for value engineering as an additional service. Custom and practice vary. Large practices may add an additional time charge for both the negotiations and the value engineering. However, small and micro-practices working for domestic clients sometimes find it difficult to do this; in part, because the client is relying on the architect's advice, which then appears inaccurate! Moreover, there is an incentive at this stage to do everything possible to allow the project to proceed and act in your client's best interests.

RIBA Plan of Work Stage 5: Manufacturing and Construction

Demolition is completed and things go smoothly on site due to the architect's meticulous coordination, which takes longer to do than expected, since many of the sustainability features must be modified to accommodate the supply chain's preferences.

The coordination of the contractor-designed mechanical services also takes more time than anticipated and extends the programme by four weeks.

The client insists that the bathroom and kitchen fit-out works dovetail into the main contract. This requires the main contractor to make special provision for access. This is a high-risk strategy relying on the contractor's goodwill, with any delays being the client's responsibility. This arrangement also involves the architect in time spent coordinating. This is made more difficult, since neither the architect nor the contactor has formal control over the client's tradespeople.

There are a number of minor client variations that add to the Construction Cost and delay the works. As a result, the construction contract programme is delayed by a total of 12 weeks, for which the contractor is granted an extension of time and the completion date is extended.

Note: The lump sum fee for Stage 5 was based on the building contract period referred to in the Project Resources Programme (and which the contractor tendered for). By treating the Project Resources Programme as a 'baseline' and keeping accurate records of person hours spent, the architect is able to claim for the additional time needed for contract administration, site inspections, and so on. It would be prudent for the architect to advise the client as to the likelihood of any additional fees as soon as the practice becomes aware of the delay and before the contractor makes its claim for a 12-week extension. Unfortunately, the client is going to be upset by the delay and not in the best frame of mind to accept additional fees!

RIBA Plan of Work Stage 6: Handover

Practical Completion is achieved and the client takes occupation. The Health and Safety File is handed over and Principal Designer duties discharged.

The client subsequently reports a leak and resultant damage to surrounding finishes. This, it transpires, is due to faulty workmanship by the client's own kitchen contractor. The architect is involved in spending time to sort out the problem on a goodwill basis.

Summary

The practice was keen to undertake the project and felt the client to be reasonable, so assessed the risk as low.

The local contractors priced Passivhaus, retaining wall and other features at a higher rate than originally estimated.

A value engineering exercise was undertaken at the architect's expense in terms of resources because the practice was embarrassed by the high tender returns and concerned that the client might abort the project. (The client could have been within their rights had they chosen to withhold fees, given that the architect had failed to deliver tenders in line with the budget.)

Removing the kitchen and bathroom from the contract required goodwill from the main contractor in allowing access onto the site and created many grey areas in terms of liability and health and safety. The subsequent leak caused damage and resolving the ensuing dispute involved the architect in a considerable amount of time, despite it not being their responsibility.

In terms of use of resources, everything went well up to RIBA Plan of Work Stage 3 (Figure 8.2, page 113). Stage 4 demanded more time than expected for coordination. The value engineering exercise also resulted in extra time being spent on the project. Taking the kitchen and bathroom out of the contract likewise involved more professional time being spent by the practice, not less.

There were several points in the Project Resources Programme where the practice could have charged additional fees, totalling 168 additional hours. For example:

- additional design development and client variation (42 hours recorded)
- value engineering (42 hours recorded)
- the 12-week extension to the construction programme (84 hours recorded).

A post-contract reality check would indicate that the fee, expressed as a percentage of the final Construction Cost (including kitchen and bathroom), represents about 10%. This is much lower than the 13% originally anticipated.

Using the break-even point and adding contingency plus profit allowed the practice to make an informed judgment as to whether to accept these additional costs or consider passing them on and making a claim for additional fees. The broad risk contingency estimate is there to absorb the sorts of costs referred to above. However, the practice had already reduced their profit and risk allowance from 35% down to 25%. The break-even costs allow the practice to see the effect that absorbing the extra costs has on the profit.

Additional design development

The practice quoted lump sum fees for the RIBA Plan of Work stages. It is likely that the practice will choose to absorb additional design development and coordination costs, as these are broadly within their control. The decision would be informed by the change management register. Unless the scope changed significantly and this was referred to in the agreement, the client will consider that this risk should be borne by the practice, requiring these costs be absorbed from the risk contingency allowance.

Value engineering

Historically, this is where projects may change or the procurement route switch from traditional to design and build, or the client look to make significant changes to the scope rather than the specification. In this case, the practice absorbs these costs (42 hours at the break-even rate, utilising all their risk contingency). The practice has also to negotiate with the engineers for the extra time they spent due to value engineering, seeing they were appointed as subconsultants.

Twelve-week extension to the building contract period

The lump sum fee was based on an estimated building contract period. The contractor agreed to this period when tendering for the works. It has now been extended by 12 weeks. The practice spent an additional 84 hours administering the contract over this period. Absorbing these costs will directly affect profit. Stage 5 was always identified as high-risk and outside the architect's control.

It makes sense to advise the client, at the earliest stage through cost reporting, of the effect of any delay on the total project costs – including fees. Stage 5 is a significant risk. If you had agreed to a lump sum without having a programme period as a qualification, then you would have to absorb the cost – and possibly move into deficit.

Good Practice Guide: Fees

Months	1	2	3	4	5	6	7	8	9	10	11	12	13	14	15	16	17	18	19	20	21	22	23	24	25	26	27	Use	Total
0 Strategic Definition (completed)																													
1 Preparation and Briefing																													
2 Concept Design																													
3 Spatial Coordination (Core statutory process)																													
4 Technical Design (Procurement route)																													
5 Manufacturing and Construction																													
6 Handover																													
7 Use																													
Person day allowance planned	4	4	10	20	10	1	1	20	40	20	4	4	4	4	4	4	4	4	4	4	4	4	0	0	0	0	0	4	182
Break-even cost (£000s)	1.6	1.6	4	8	4	0.4	0.4	8	16	8	1.6	1.6	1.6	1.6	1.6	1.6	1.6	1.6	1.6	1.6	1.6	1.6	0	0	0	0	0	1.6	72.8
Profit + Risk 25% planned	0.4	0.4	1	2	1	0.1	0.1	2	4	2	0.4	0.4	0.4	0.4	0.4	0.4	0.4	0.4	0.4	0.4	0.4	0.4	0	0	0	0	0	0.4	18.2
Total fee (£000s)	2	2	5	10	5	0.5	0.5	10	20	10	2	2	2	2	2	2	2	2	2	2	2	2	0	0	0	0	0	2	91
Fee per RIBA stage (£000s)	(1) 2	(2) 2	(3) 21				(4) 44							(5+6) 20													(7) 2		91
Monthly fee instalments (£000s)	2	2	4	4	4	5	8	9	9	9	2	2	2	2	2	2	2	2	2	2	2	2						2	91

▼ CLIENT MEETING
■ DESIGN TEAM MEETING
▲ CONTRACTOR MEETING

PLANNING APPLICATION
TENDER
MOBILISATION
DEMOLITIONS

Notes: Break-even costs are based on £400 per day as office finance calculation.
Charge out rate used for fee calculation is based on the negotiated fee, which included 20% for profit and risk resulting in £500 per day.

Figure 8.1: Project Resources Programme with planned person days

Putting it into practice: a case study 8

Months	1	2	3	4	5	6	7	8	9	10	11	12	13	14	15	16	17	18	19	20	21	22	23	24	25	26	27	Use	Total
0 Strategic Definition (completed)																													
1 Preparation and Briefing																													
2 Concept Design																													
3 Spatial Coordination (Core statutory process)																													
4 Technical Design (Procurement route)																													
5 Manufacturing and Construction																													
6 Handover																													
7 Use																													
Person day allowance planned	4	4	10	20	10	1	1	20	40	20	4	4	4	4	4	4	4	4	4	4	4	4	0	0	0	0	0	4	182
Break-even cost (£000s)	1.6	1.6	4	8	4	0.4	0.4	8	16	8	1.6	1.6	1.6	1.6	1.6	1.6	1.6	1.6	1.6	1.6	1.6	1.6	0	0	0	0	0	1.6	72.8
Profit + Risk 25% planned	0.4	0.4	1	2	1	0.1	0.1	2	4	2	0.4	0.4	0.4	0.4	0.4	0.4	0.4	0.4	0.4	0.4	0.4	0.4	0	0	0	0	0	0.4	18.2
Total fee (£000s)	2	2	5	10	5	0.5	0.5	10	20	10	2	2	2	2	2	2	2	2	2	2	2	2	0	0	0	0	0	2	91
Person days actually spent	5	5	12	22	10	2	2	20	40	20	4	10	5	4	4	4	4	4	4	4	4	4	4	4	4	4	4	4	217
Actual staff cost incurred based on break-even rates	2	2	4.8	8.8	4	0.8	0.8	8	16	8	1.6	4	2	1.6	1.6	1.6	1.6	1.6	1.6	1.6	1.6	1.6	1.6	1.6	1.6	1.6	1.6	1.6	86.4
Actual profit (£000s)	0	0	0.2	1.2	1	-0.3	-0.3	2	4	2	0.4	-2	0	0.4	0.4	0.4	0.4	0.4	0.4	0.4	0.4	0.4	-1.6	-1.6	-1.6	-1.6	-1.6	0.4	4.2
Cumulative actual profit (£000s)	0	0	0.2	1.4	2.4	2.1	1.8	3.8	7.8	9.8	10.2	8.2	8.2	8.6	9.0	9.4	9.8	10.2	10.6	11.0	11.4	11.8	10.2	8.6	7.0	5.4	3.8	4.2	4.2

Notes: Break-even costs are based on £400 per day as office finance calculation.
Charge out rate used for fee calculation is based on the negotiated fee, which included 20% for profit and risk resulting in £500 per day.

Figure 8.2: Project Resources Programme with actual person days spent

WATCH POINTS

- It is important to keep on top of budgeted estimates for the design as it develops. Otherwise, value engineering design work may end up being undertaken at your practice's expense in terms of office resources.

- If you employ subconsultants, not only are you responsible for their performance in terms of liability, you may also have to deal with any fee claims, if the scope of work changes or the subconsultants are involved in extra work (e.g. in value engineering).

- Underestimating the ability of small-scale contractors to deal with bespoke detailing can result in high tenders.

- The client should be cautioned and reminded about the level of accuracy of pre-tender estimates.

- Not communicating late design development changes to the cost consultant (in this case, the bathroom and kitchen specifications) can result in inaccurate budget estimates.

- It is possible to underestimate the amount of time required to handle the design as it develops at Stages 1 to 3. An end-of-stage design sign-off system can help.

- If the actual person days spent delivering the service total more than planned, this data should be fed back into the practice records for reference when preparing future fee proposals.

- The Project Resources Programme can be used to show planned and actual resources. This allows the practice to take an informed view on the implications of additional work and discuss any additional fees with the client in a timely manner.

9

Summary

It's all about time. Delivering a professional service while running a sustainable practice depends on how you build an initial fee proposal; how you create a professional services contract with your client; and how you monitor the project. It is important to understand the market sectors you are working in and your own unique selling points, as they affect commercial decisions about profit and risk. Using financial data from your own business to calculate your break-even point will help run a viable and professional practice.

The fees you charge and how you manage projects are critical to viability. If you want to stay in practice, your business must be economically sustainable. The legacy of the percentage fee is both a curse and a blessing to the profession. Using your own practice data on percentage fees charged in the past is a useful way of carrying out a reality check. However, even the most experienced practitioners agree that calculating a fee based solely on a percentage of the construction cost can lead to wildly differing levels of profit (and loss) on projects.

There is a culture within some sectors of the profession of accepting these fluctuations in profit, because otherwise making any claim for extra fees could jeopardise the chances of getting another job from the same client. Yet, this approach to charging is not found in other industries (including, of course, general contracting), where businesses expect to be reimbursed for the work they do. If the client or customer changes their brief, there will be a cost implication. The purpose of this guide has been to encourage you to think about how you set out your professional services contract and the method of charging for your services. If you then choose to take a more relaxed view on a particular project's profitability, you will do so from an informed perspective.

Your sector and specialisms

Chapter 1 described the different procurement routes used for building projects, the risks associated with the different RIBA Plan of Work stages and how to mitigate those risks by creating clear boundaries in terms of cost and time. The limitations of benchmarking data have been pointed out in Chapter 3, suggesting that it is safer to rely on your own practice's historical data. Information contained within benchmarking data can, however, be useful when comparing the work you are doing and the fees you charge with those of competitors. Chapter 3 also discussed the research that may be required when entering new sectors. The level of fees and charging methods can vary enormously from sector to sector. It may simply not be viable for, say, a large commercial practice to work in the social housing sector. Understanding your own specialisms and how you sit alongside your competitors is important, and you should take every opportunity to obtain feedback on fee levels to supplement your own office data.

Your business model

The essence of any fee proposal is the charge out rate. Understanding how you arrived at the rate, how your business model works and what your break-even point is are all critical. Knowing these facts boosts confidence when putting a fee proposal together. Software packages can reduce the burden of dealing with figures and the financial management of the business. It is, nevertheless, important to be familiar with the basic principles underpinning these systems. Many practitioners have been schooled in percentage fees, and sometimes fail to consider the true costs to the practice when putting together a fee proposal. Understanding your own business model, attitude to risk, working capital and future aspirations will inform the way you charge for your service. Only by making a profit are you able to invest in the future. Having a positive bank balance, rather than an overdraft, gives the freedom to pursue initiatives and develop the practice in the future. Bidding for work estimated on low profit margins increases risk, leaving little room for manoeuvre when things go wrong.

Summary | 9

The Project Resources Programme

The Project Resources Programme ties everything together. As described in Chapter 4, this document should be developed during initial client negotiations and form part of your professional services contract. Once up and running, it provides a datum allowing you to monitor a project in terms of resources and progress. The form and detail of the document can vary, depending upon the size and complexity of the project. It is particularly useful where a partial service is being provided; for example, when commissioned by a domestic client for RIBA Plan of Work Stages 1 to 3 only. It can be produced as a rough, hand-drawn programme or a more sophisticated bar chart using computer software. Whatever system you choose, by sharing the document with the client, it serves as a useful tool for discussing requirements in an objective way. The Project Resources Programme also provides a basis for managing your office resources. You may choose not to disclose your office person day allowances to the client, but a programme with key dates is a useful document and provides a datum against which any future changes can be compared. In addition, by sharing the Project Resources Programme with your staff, you involve them in the overall plan and thereby ensure their buy-in to the management and resourcing of the project.

Monitoring resources

To optimise the performance of your practice by receiving feedback and gaining insight it is essential that project resources are monitored. It is strongly advised that you regularly monitor what is happening with your projects, while at the same time understanding how well your business is performing overall. Every project you design is a prototype. Unexpected incidents can happen. Some changes, events and developments can be accommodated within your original fee agreement, but this is often not the case. The additional work required by a project can have a serious impact on the office resources. Keeping track of such changes and monitoring the person days expended requires simple and robust monitoring systems, both to flag up any problems and to have the evidence to back up discussions concerning the fee implications with the client, if necessary.

Keeping the client informed is paramount. It is neither professional nor sensible to try to negotiate additional fees at the end of a project. Even for a modestly sized project, understanding the mechanism of change control and keeping the client informed is crucial. Chapter 4 stresses the value of empathy and seeing a situation from the client's perspective. Being able to provide evidence of additional work, rather than just referring to office time sheets, will help support your case. Maintaining an overview of the whole office and all projects is also important. This way, the overspend of resources on one job can be balanced by the profitability of others.

The importance of cash

As stated in Chapter 7, cash is king – without it, your practice cannot survive. The majority of practices prepare cash flow forecasts. These give them a reasonable idea of how, for example, the next six months are likely to pan out. When approaching invoicing and terms of appointment, think about your working capital and what sort of financial safety net you need. Monitoring any lag in cash flow, regardless of whether the practice happens to be expanding or contracting, is important if nasty surprises are to be avoided. Having an overview of the amount of revenue required for the forthcoming year puts into perspective the ups and down of individual projects in terms of the overall office finances.

Invoicing and payment

The need for regular invoicing has been addressed in Chapter 7. Stating invoicing points, preferably monthly ones, at the outset is a vital component of your professional services contract. The submission of regular fee invoices produces a steadier income flow. Tying payments into the RIBA Plan of Work stages can create cash flow problems and increase the likelihood of delays in payment. This can be because there are delays to the completion of a particular stage, or because the client is slow in signing off the design prior to a planning submission. Monthly payments are far safer and are likely to tie in with the client's finance systems. The level and frequency of invoicing could also take account of the risk profile of the client, particularly as regards the final invoice, where the risk of non-payment is often highest. In some instances, payment in advance of carrying out the initial design work would be a sensible option, especially with a new client.

Adding value and your unique selling point (USP)

Throughout this guide, the importance of appreciating where you add value to a project has been emphasised, whether it be obtaining planning permission in challenging circumstances or creating a design with greater efficiencies for the client's operation. Chapter 4 underlined that the professional services contract between a client and an architect has to be to the benefit of both parties. Any added value should be reflected in the charge out rate when calculating the fee. This is why it is recommended that you calculate your fee net of profit and then add an appropriate sum to reflect the level of skill required and the added value for the client. Although familiarity with a sector means you can work efficiently and minimise the risk to your client, such expertise is likely to have been acquired through many years of hard-earned professional experience, and this ought to be reflected in your fee.

Summary

Every firm of architects is different, not just in size, but also the sector worked in and the philosophy underpinning the practice. There is no one-size-fits-all approach to either fees or business management. That said, the general principle of calculating fees in a methodical manner and then monitoring those fees against the Project Resources Programme is an important discipline. Even should you choose to charge a percentage of the construction cost or some type of incentive fee, the process of calculating a fee relative to a Project Resources Programme and your estimated resource costs allows you to establish whether the fee is viable and where the risks might be. It also means you can monitor the project against an agreed datum and this helps to ensure that you and your practice get properly reimbursed for the work that you do. We all aspire to create good quality design. Following the strategy outlined in this guide should help make your projects not only successful but also profitable.

INDEX

Note: page numbers in italics refer to figures; page numbers in bold refer to tables.

added value 50–51, 54, 57, 70, 91, 118
additional fees 27–28, 67, 69, 80, 90, 93
approvals and permissions 23
    see also planning applications and consents
ARB: The Architects Code 21, 68

benchmarking information 31–36, 57
bespoke contracts 24–25
break-even point 52
budget *see* project budget
building contract *see* procurement routes
business model 116

case study 99–114
    feasibility study 100–104
    fee estimation 104–105
    Project Resources Programme *112*, *113*
    RIBA Professional Services Contract (PSC) 105–107
    work stages 107–109
cash flow 74, 118
    forecast 75–76, **76, 77**, 88
change control 68–69, 81, 90, 92
changes
    to contract 27–28
    to procurement strategy 65
    to project scope 66, 80, 89, 94–95
charge out rates 32, 35
    average charge out rates by practice size **35**
    average hourly charge out rates *34*
    calculation 36–40, **101**
charging methods 44–47, 56
client adviser role 3, 56
client communication 65–66, 80, 91
    see also project review meetings
client representative 10
client risks 4
collaborative procurement 13–14
communication *see* client communication; project review meetings
complaints procedure 91
construction contract *see* procurement routes
construction costs 93
Construction Industry Council (CIC) novation agreement 25
construction management 12–13
construction risks 6
construction stage 94, 109
consultant switch 10
consultants 23, 49–50
    see also subconsultants
consumer clients *see* domestic clients
Consumer Rights Act 2015 (CRA 2015) 21, 22
contract administrator 3, 93–94
contract performance 6, 19
contractor risks 6
copyright 88–89
cost risk 5, 52, 54, 61, 88

delays
    affecting cash flow 75

affecting resource plan 89
cost risk 46, 68
responsibility for 90
design and build procurement 9, 24, 25–26
design development 90–92
design liability 19, 49–50
design risks 5
developer clients 11, 24, 56
dispute resolution 97
domestic clients 22, 26–27, 28
drawings 25

expenses 23, 47, 54

feasibility studies 56, 80, 100–104
fee calculation 51–57
    see also charge out rates; charging methods
fee negotiation 58–60, 61, 105
fee payments *see* payments
fee proposal 17, 27, 51–56
    adding value 51
    case study 104
    entering new sectors 57
    exclusions 55
    partial services 56–57
fee risks 27–28
fees, zero 89
framework agreements 13–14

general contracting 8–9

health and safety adviser 3
health and safety risks 6–7

interim payments 86
invoicing 85–86
    timing 23, 86–87, 118

late payment 95–97
lead designer 3
legal advice 24
letter contracts 23–24, 87
letters of comfort 27
letters of intent 26
lump sum contracts 44–45, 56, 61, 89

management contracting 12, 24
meetings *see* project review meetings
monitoring progress 73–74
monitoring resources 79–80, 117–118

negotiation 58–60, 61
non-payment 60
novation 9–10, 25–26

office finances 31–41, **101**
    office performance 70
    profit margin *33*, 38, 52, 54, 68, 70
    whole office resource issues 69–70, 75
    see also cash flow; charge out rates; profit margin
oral agreements 20

partial services 56–57, 86

Good Practice Guide: Fees

payments
    late 95–97
    non-payment 60
    timing 23, 25, 86–87, 118
percentage fees 36, 45–46, 89, 115
planning applications and consents 23, 66, 70, 89
planning negotiations 67, 92
post-contract stage 19
practice finances see office finances
pre-contract stage 19, 22, 26–27
Principal Designer 23, 28
procurement routes 1–2, 8–14
    design and build 9, 24, 25–26
    effect of changes to strategy 65, 94–95
    management contracting 12, 24
    resource implications 67
    traditional contracting 8–9, 45, 47, 49
professional indemnity insurance (PII) 24, 49, 54
professional services contracts (PSCs) 2, 17–29
    bespoke contracts 24–25
    changes 27–28
    contract performance 19
    letter contracts 23–24
    post-contract stage 19
    pre-contract stage 19, 22
    as a project 18
    standard contracts 22–23
    terms of contract 19
profit benchmarking 32, 33
profit margin 33, 38, 52, 54, 68, 70
profitability indicator 76–79, **78, 79**
progress monitoring 73–74
project budget 65
project characteristics 2, 4, 15, 22
project manager 3
project programme 23
Project Resources Programme 64–65, 67, 117
    as basis for fee calculation 52
    bespoke contracts 24
    case study 112, 113
    effect of delays 46
    example 53
    monitoring progress 73–74
    outputs 52, 55
    timescales 22
project review meetings 52, 65–66, 79–80
project risks 3–7, 14
project roles 3
project scope 2
project timescales 22

regulatory risks 5–6
resource allocation 68
    see also Project Resources Programme
resources monitoring 79–80, 117–18
resources planning 64, 68, 69–70, 79, 81
responsibility matrix 26
revenue benchmarking 32, 33
review meetings see project review meetings
RIBA Business Benchmarking survey 31, 32
RIBA Code of Professional Conduct 2019 20

RIBA Plan of Work 2020 2–3
    construction management 12–13
    design and build 10–11
    management contracting 12
    partial services 56
    roles 3
    traditional contracting 8–9
    work stages and methods of charging **48**, 55
    work stages and project risks **48**, 52, 67, 70
    work stages and value added 51
RIBA Professional Services Contracts (PSCs) 22–23
    Concise PSC 22
    design team appointments 49
    Domestic PSC 22, 28, 105–107
    fee adjustment 89–90
    fee payments 86
    key dates 64
    Principal Designer PSC 28
    risk transfer 27–28
    Subconsultant PSC 49, 105
risk allocation 24, 26, 27–28, 89
risk assessment 15, 47, **48**
risk management 7, 27–28, 61
risk premium 26, 27, 89
roles 3

schedule of services 23
site risks 5
software 65
specialist services 56, 57
staff resources planning 64, 68, 69–70, 79, 81
stage payments 118
standard contracts 22–23
statutory fees 54
subconsultants 49–50
    case study 105
    and design liability 49–50
    management and liability costs 54
    management of 49–50
'subject to contract' 26
substitution 51

tax 32
termination of contract 25
terms of appointment 19, 20, 21
    see also professional services contracts (PSCs)
time charges 46–47, 89
time management 66
timescales 22
traditional contracting 8–9, 45, 47, 49
two-stage tendering 93

unique selling point (USP) 118–119

value see added value
value engineering 93, 108, 111
variations see changes

whole office resource issues 69–70, 75
working capital 74, 84–85

zero fees 89

122